Alfredo Catalani
Composer of Lucca

Alfredo Catalani, 1890

Alfredo Catalani
Composer of Lucca

Domenico Luigi Pardini

With Firsthand Accounts of Catalani by
Giovanni Baptista Nappi
and Raffaello Barbiera

Edited, annotated, and introduced by
David Chandler

Translated by Valentina Relton

First published in this form by Durrant Publishing, 2010

Hardback   ISBN 978-1-905946-15-0
Paperback ISBN 978-1-905946-09-9

First Edition

Enquiries have been made to discover whether there is anyone who might claim copyright in Domenico Luigi Pardini's *Alfredo Catalani: Quaderno di Ricordi Lucchesi* (1935), but these came to nothing. Should this translation come to the attention of anyone who does lay claim to the copyright, the editor will be pleased to discuss the matter with them. We believe that Pardini published his book with no view to personal profit, but simply to extend the fame of Alfredo Catalani; this translation is issued in the same spirit.

∞ The paper used in this publication meets the minimum requirements of the American National Standard for Information Sciences – Permanence of Paper for Printed Library Materials, ANSI Z39.48-1992. The paper is acid-free and lignin-free.

Printed and bound by Lightning Source
Published by Durrant Publishing
82 Earlham Road, Norwich, NR2 3HA

For Ann Ashizu and Mariella Checkley
'O, how they sing!'

Domenico Luigi Pardini (1864–1951) lived in Lucca all his life, studying at the Istituto Musicale Pacini and later establishing a reputation as a distinguished local historian with a special interest in the city's musical heritage. He spent many years researching the first full critical biography of Alfredo Catalani, originally published in 1935.

Valentina Relton is an independent translator working in London. Her website is at: http://www.expressit.org/

David Chandler is an Associate Professor in the English Department at Doshisha University, Kyoto. His website is at: http://www.davidjchandler.co.uk/

Contents

Acknowledgements

SEVERAL PEOPLE have made this book possible; we warmly thank them all. Roberto Gollo of the Biblioteca Nazionale Braidense located and scanned the invaluable article by Giovanni Battista Nappi translated here. Michela Graziani, Vice President of the Circolo Amici della Musica Alfredo Catalani, tracked down biographical information concerning Domenico Luigi Pardini, besides offering general encouragement. Hans C. Reinders, a great Catalani collector, was generous with his time and knowledge, and the illustrations reproduced inside this book are from his collection of memorabilia associated with the composer. Maarten Ruijters generously allowed us to reproduce as a cover illustration the delightful drawing of San Martino, Lucca, from his travel sketchbook. Paul Durrant has been an amazing publisher, taking enormous care in page setting a difficult text. The biggest thanks of all must go to Giulia Martino, who with infinite patience advised on many difficulties in the translation. Giulia also translated the extracts from Carlo Paladini's 1903 article published here.

Acknowledgements of a different kind are due to the many singers, musicians, conductors, impresarios and recording companies who have made Catalani's music a living legacy; thanks to them, the subject of this book is not of merely 'academic interest.'

List of Illustrations

---

1 The original photograph from which this image was printed is reproduced in Alfredo Bonaccorsi, *Alfredo Catalani* (Turin, 1942), plate 18. Bonaccorsi dates it to 1890.

2 The provenance of this portrait is mysterious. It appears to have been first reproduced in *Nel Centenario della Nascita di Alfredo Catalani* (Lucca, 1954), 37, where, however, it appears in a circular form. No date or artist's name is given, and the picture is simply described as 'The Final Portrait of Catalani.' The postcard image reproduced here was very likely published at around the same time. An obviously related portrait in the Oratorio della Madonnina in Lucca is reproduced in *Alfredo Catalani: Nel Centocinquantesimo Anniversario della Nascita (1854-2004)* (Lucca, 2004), 190. Again no artist's name is given. Either one image derives from the other, or both derive from a common, lost source; both are probably posthumous.

ix

Introduction:
Puccini's Great Rival

David Chandler

IN THE final volume of his monumental trilogy, *The Operas of Verdi*, Julian Budden states:

> Whether if he had lived [Alfredo] Catalani would have overtaken his fellow-Luccan Puccini as the front-runner of the 'giovane scuola' can only be guessed. Certain of their contemporaries, notably [Arturo] Toscanini, thought that Catalani had the finer sensibility of the two.[1]

Such a comment will surprise – perhaps astonish – the many people who consider household-name Puccini securely established at the centre of the modern operatic repertoire, while knowing nothing of his 'fellow-Luccan.' Yet Catalani's music, though obviously much less well known than Puccini's, has proved of enduring value, its beauty and power frequently surprising and delighting those who have taken the trouble to listen. Thus such a sensitive and informed opera critic as David McKee, reviewing some recordings of *La Wally* (1892), Catalani's last opera, a few years ago, found himself disagreeing with the conventional conclusions of operatic history:

---

1 *The Operas of Verdi 3: From* Don Carlos *to* Falstaff (London and New York, 1981), 289–90.

> The more one delves into it [*La Wally*], the more
> one recognizes why Arturo Toscanini esteemed
> its composer over Puccini. ... Had Catalani
> lived beyond his too-brief allotment of years
> (1854–1893), he would have emerged as a more
> plausible bearer of the Verdian standard than
> Puccini.[1]

Noting the increasingly international style of Italian opera in the late 1800s, McKee goes on to praise Catalani's intelligent and sensitive assimilation of German influences: '*La Wally* displays a more convincing synthesis of the German and Italian styles than do any of Puccini's scores ... *La Wally* stands astride the Alps.'[2]

There is no need to agree, or to think that some sort of choice between the two composers must be made: Puccini *and* Catalani is surely preferable to Puccini *or* Catalani. But given Puccini's domination of the modern stage, the lazy, widespread assumption that success in art is a measure of merit, and the stale half-truths which have all too often allowed Catalani to be dismissed as a transitional figure, it is always refreshing to hear a sensible case made for the older composer. It was Catalani, after all, that Verdi famously described as 'a good man and excellent musician!'[3] Less well known is Puccini's own tribute to the 'fellow-Luccan' he had seen as a dangerous rival. In 1900 he hailed Catalani as a 'distinguished and original composer,' a 'glorious yet unfortunate artist,' 'a lasting memory etched into the soul of any Italian endowed with an appreciation and love for all things tender and poetic.'[4]

---

1 'Tebaldi in *La Wally*,' *Opera Quarterly* 13 (1997), 195.

2 Ibid. 195–96.

3 See below, pp. 78, 103, 131.

4 *Onoranze al maestro Alfredo Catalani* (Lucca, 1900), 14.

Catalani and Puccini emerged as composers at a time of perceived crisis in Italian opera. That crisis, as Alan Mallach has suggested, can be traced back to around 1860, when Verdi began slowing down.[1] By that time Italian opera had been a potent cultural force in Europe for well over two centuries. The previous fifty years had been particularly rich, with Rossini, Bellini, Donizetti, and Verdi producing a string of masterpieces that formed the basis of the modern Italian repertoire, as well as satisfying the demand for Italian opera abroad. But with Bellini and Donizetti long dead, and Rossini long retired, by 1860 the future of the genre lay almost entirely with Verdi, leading to what Lorenzo Bianconi has called 'a sort of "father complex" in the Italian musical world.'[2] But the formerly prolific Verdi wrote only two operas in the 1860s and just one in the 1870s (all for foreign theatres), and for many years it seemed that *Aida* (1871) would be his last. There was no one to inherit his mantle, and with the increasing international success of French and German opera, even in Italy, Italians began to feel anxious about the future of a musical genre they had created and long dominated. Leadership passed to Amilcare Ponchielli, whose *La Gioconda*, premiered in 1876 and exhaustively revised in the following years, remains by far the best-known Italian opera from the decade after *Aida*. But Ponchielli was slightly extending the possibilities of Verdian opera rather than creating anything really new, and his later operas enjoyed only a very limited success in Italy and none abroad. He was not an answer to the problem, and as the 1880s dawned there was an increasing sense of crisis, as well as great opportunities for a young composer with fresh ideas. First Catalani, and later Puccini and others, took up the challenge of refashioning Italian opera, building on Italian traditions, but opening them to foreign influences.

------

1 *Pietro Mascagni and His Operas* (Boston, 2002), 62.

2 'Italy' in *The New Grove Dictionary of Opera*.

Because Catalani and Puccini were born just four years apart, and both grew up in Lucca, comparison has, at least since 1893, been inevitable. But it is necessary, indeed important, to bring some sort of historical perspective to bear on a relationship that has too often been viewed very unhistorically, with Puccini's eventual 'triumph' taken as a starting point, and Catalani then tucked into a subsidiary relationship. It was Catalani who blossomed sooner, establishing himself in the mid-1870s as 'a new and original talent with a radical approach to music drama,'[1] and for a time he was a powerful influence and inspiration for his 'fellow-Luccan': Puccini's first opera, *Le Villi* (1884), is shot through with Catalani's influence at every level. In fact as late as Catalani's final premiere, *La Wally* in 1892, his absolute ascendancy was undeniable. By that time he had seen five full-length operas produced, the latter three – *Edmea* (1886), *Loreley* (1890), and *La Wally* – all substantial and steadily increasing successes. Puccini, by contrast, had produced just one full-length opera, *Edgar* (1889), and that had proved a disaster. The great success of Puccini's *Manon Lescaut* in 1893 – Puccini was by then 34 – created a genuine and meaningful rivalry, and had Catalani been in good health a fascinating and probably mutually beneficial battle of styles and ideas might have been fought out in the following years, prompting Julian Budden's open question about which of these immensely talented men would then have emerged as the 'front-runner' among the young Italian composers. But just seven months after the premiere of *Manon*, Catalani succumbed to the tuberculosis he had struggled with throughout his adult life. At his death he had planned another opera that would have represented his artistic response to Puccini's mature style; none of it, sadly, was put down on paper.

Given the personal and artistic relationship between Catalani and Puccini, one might reasonably expect the latter's centrality

---

1 Budden, *Operas of Verdi 3*, 286.

in the modern operatic repertoire to work to Catalani's advantage. Yet it does not seem to have done so, for reasons I tend to think of as the Mosco Carner effect. Carner's very successful and unquestionably important *Puccini: A Critical Biography*, first published in 1958, included the most in-depth portrait of Catalani attempted in any English publication at that time and long after. Before Carner, the English reader looking for information on Catalani had to make do with encyclopedic works, and 'How brief and perfunctory are the references to Catalani in all the musical dictionaries!' John W. Klein, a notable champion, had lamented in 1937.[1] Carner's four pages on Catalani are remarkable for three things: (a) they say virtually nothing about Catalani's music; (b) they discuss Catalani almost entirely in his relation to Puccini; and (c) they present as negative an image of Catalani the man as a responsible scholar could go without actually distorting the evidence.[2] Yet Carner's account starts promisingly enough. He notes that Puccini admired Catalani's *Dejanice* (1883), that in the early 1880s Catalani was 'the great hope of Italian opera,' that Toscanini preferred Catalani's music to Puccini's, and that Puccini 'often visited' Catalani in his student days, reporting the older composer 'most kind' – all this in half a page.[3] Rather than discussing what would seem naturally to follow, the influence of Catalani on Puccini, however, he then tacked off in a different direction:

---

1 'Alfredo Catalani,' *Musical Quarterly* 23 (1937), 287.

2 It is worth noting, though, that Carner buttressed his essentially anti-Catalani case with extended quotations from two letters, attributed to Verdi, which in Carner's judgment were of 'very doubtful' authenticity. One can reasonably question why a scholar would make a good deal of documents that he considered inauthentic. The letters in question spitefully refer to Catalani as 'that little master of Lucca [*maestrino lucchese*],' with his 'German opera[s].'

3 *Puccini: A Critical Biography* (London, 1958), 28.

> But this friendly relationship [between Catalani
> and Puccini] subsequently deteriorated into an
> ill-concealed hostility on the part of the older
> composer when Puccini ... was taken up by
> Giulio Ricordi, then head of the great firm of
> Milan music publishers [in 1884], and when
> Catalani's own operas were beginning to be
> overshadowed by those of his fellow-Lucchese
> [in 1893].

The reader is then asked to 'take a jump forward in time, to
the period between 1889 and 1893 when Puccini's *Edgar* and
Manon Lescaut had already been composed.' (The dates are
rather indiscriminately mixed up.) Carner devotes most of his
remaining pages to demonstrating Catalani's 'hostility' and
'bitter jealousy' through extended quotations from the composer's letters to Giuseppe Depanis (which had recently been
published in Italian).

One does not need to excuse Catalani on the grounds of
chronic ill health and the blatant favouritism Ricordi showed
Puccini to find something unpleasant and unfair in hurry-
ing the reader on from any contemplation of that erstwhile
'friendly relationship' and judging a man on the basis of the
most 'bitter' things he may have vented to a close friend in
private correspondence.[1] At the same time, of course, saying nothing about Puccini's role in any bad feeling that may

---

1 Catalani wrote revealingly to Depanis on 26 November 1892: 'I know
that with you, at least, I can say everything that I think, everything beautiful, ugly, good, bad that passes through my head. Unfortunately, these
days the ugly triumphs over the beautiful, and then I burst out in lamenta-
tions, which you understand, but which would come out as unbearable
to someone else.' *The Politics of Opera in Turn-of-the-Century Italy: As Seen
Through the Letters of Alfredo Catalani*, trans. and ed. Richard M. Berrong
(Lampeter, 1992), 122.

have developed between the two composers.[1] But the worst of it is that all this material essentially stands in for any other account of a composer who was clearly personally and professionally important to Puccini, as though to say 'this is Catalani: he was hostile, bitter, jealous. A bad loser, and someone who deserved to lose.' The association with Puccini, rather than becoming a reason for interest, was thus turned against Catalani, and though Carner was probably not the first and certainly not the last to do this, his account has, arguably, been the most influential, not just in the English-speaking world, but pretty much everywhere else, too: his book was translated into French, Italian, German, Spanish, and even Japanese. The long shadow of Catalani's supposedly poisonous jealousy has lain heavy over many subsequent accounts of the composer.

Remarkably, though, Carner's lop-sided and obviously tendentious picture of Puccini's great rival was very much at odds with the conclusions of Catalani's Italian biographers. The first of these, Giuseppe Depanis, the recipient of those very letters that Carner built his case on, and a great admirer of both composers, read in Catalani's embittered comments only the 'resigned protest of a genius aware of his own value who finds

---

1 Catalani was convinced that Puccini actively conspired against him. Referring to the recent production of *La Wally* in Lucca, he wrote to Giuseppe Depanis on 20 September 1892: 'You can't imagine, confidentially, what I suffered in Lucca because of the war that Puccini and the Mayor, his relative, waged against me.' *Letters*, ed. Berrong, 117. Catalani was a little paranoid about such matters, but it is more likely than not that there was some foundation for his accusation. He was, however, confused about his enemy: Enrico Del Carlo, the Mayor, had been a supporter of Catalani according to Domenico Luigi Pardini (see below, pp. 70, 72); his brother, Massimo Del Carlo, was Puccini's brother-in-law. It is worth reiterating that at this time Puccini, for all his great talents, had made no significant impact on the operatic world; even after he had achieved extraordinary success he was not above plotting against his rivals.

himself isolated and, worse, thwarted.'[1] They did not prevent him understanding Catalani as a noble, idealistic, dedicated, rather heroic artist, and withal a kind, gentle, congenial man. Depanis was perhaps too close to Catalani to be altogether impartial, but his view of the composer was largely shared by other early commentators, including Giovanni Battista Nappi, whose important 1918 essay is included in the present volume. Later biographers, Domenico Luigi Pardini (1935), Carlo Gatti (1953), Rinaldo Cortopassi (1954) and Severino Pagani (1957), similarly found in Catalani a man as admirable in his personal life as in his art. Commenting specifically on the Gatti and Pagani biographies, Jay Nicolaisen observes that their accounts of the composer

> could only strike us as romanticized, did they not agree at nearly every point with all the other evidence available. Catalani, it seems clear, was that rare artist who inspired admiration and trust in nearly everyone who met him.[2]

No doubt these and the other biographers did 'romanticize' and idealize a little, but Catalani's steady pursuit of his artistic goals through incapacitating illness and family tragedy (despite his early death, he had witnessed the deaths of both parents and both siblings), and in the face of hostile criticism, make his a life that is singularly easy to romanticize. The various portraits and photographs of Catalani that survive, though they painfully document his physical decline, reveal a noble, rather ethereal spirit, as different as possible from the sensual and sardonic countenance Puccini presented to the world. Indeed, Catalani's superiority to his fellow Luccan in terms of character can hardly be doubted – as Carner must have realized.

---

1 *Alfredo Catalani: Appunti – Ricordi* (Turin, 1893), 18.

2 *Italian Opera in Transition, 1871–1893* (Ann Arbor, 1980), 153.

Some will naturally question what this has to do with music. That a man with grave character flaws can be a great artist is something of a modern article of faith; conversely, there is often a cynical suspicion that too much goodness is bad for art. But in the late 1800s, when art was perhaps taken more seriously than at any time before or since, there was great interest in the moral character of the artist, and a strong belief that this was, in some way or other, tied to the value of the art. Catalani certainly believed as much, and had a very lofty and thoroughly Romantic view of his artistic calling, which brought with it a tendency to over-stress the difficulty 'true' art has in making its way in a world awash with the meretricious (he did, after all, enjoy considerable success). And early writers on Catalani, even hostile critics, recognized in him a singularly 'sincere,' 'idealistic' and 'honest' musician, the sort of vocabulary that continued to be used by his champions into the 1950s, by which time the culture that had given meaning to such attitudes had changed to the point where the words could be dismissed as critical cant. By contrast, the dying Catalani is said to have come to the conclusion that 'Puccini is not sincere. That man, I am sure, is not sincere.'[1] It is hard, no doubt, to avoid the feeling that some sour grapes lie behind the statement; nevertheless, it is only fair to Catalani to admit that many distinguished critics have expressed similar views.[2] One can agree or disagree, and one can also recognize that Catalani himself was no saint in his personal life, and not above trying to please the public, despite some of his more idealistic comments. But no Italian composer of his generation took their music more seriously than Catalani, or

---

1 John W. Klein, 'Toscanini and Catalani – A Unique Friendship,' *Music and Letters* 48 (1967), 223.

2 Joseph Kerman, for example, who in his classic study, *Opera as Drama* (New York, 1956), describes Puccini as an 'unthinking opportunist' whose operas are 'false through and through' (259, 262).

placed so much emphasis on personal style, and being true to oneself. And perhaps no other lived *for* their art in quite the way he did, or needed it so badly. Nappi quotes with approval and emphasis Depanis's judgment: '*The art he [Catalani] worshipped, despite all its disillusions, was his only defence against the pain and cruelty of life.*' At the end of the day one can only admire Catalani for his convictions and his struggles, and for the exquisite music which emerged from them.

Catalani's reputation has ebbed and flowed. In his lifetime, as noted already, he enjoyed steadily increasing success; with *La Wally* it appeared he had finally established himself as a major force in Italian opera. Unfortunately, the appearance of Verdi's *Falstaff* and Puccini's *Manon Lescaut* soon afterwards stole the limelight away from Catalani. A number of younger composers were also making their mark at just this time with the new 'verismo' style: Pietro Mascagni (in 1890), Ruggiero Leoncavallo (in 1892), and Umberto Giordano (in 1892). With so much going on, although Catalani's death was seen as a tragedy for Italian music, it did not lead to a renewed interest in his operas. Over the following decade he was gradually forgotten. Around 1904, however, with the verismo bubble having burst, there began a remarkable revival of interest in Catalani's work, as Thomas G. Kaufman's wonderful performance catalogue, *Verdi and His Major Contemporaries* (New York and London, 1990), makes clear.[1] In the following two decades not only were there dozens of productions of *Loreley* and *La Wally*, but even the early *Dejanice* (1883) experienced a extraordinary burst of productions after its revival in Turin in 1920, and *Edmea* was not wholly forgotten, with productions in Turin in 1910 and Modena in 1914. This was the golden age for Catalani in the theatre.

---

1 John Klein regards 'the turning of the tide' as occurring when Toscanini conducted *La Wally* with great success in Buenos Aires in summer 1904. 'Toscanini and Catalani,' 226.

The most important literary products of this Catalani revival were substantial biographical and critical articles on the composer by Carlo Gatti (his first important writing on Catalani) and Giovanni Battista ('G. B.') Nappi. These were both published in 1918, to mark the twenty-fifth anniversary of Catalani's death. Nappi's four-part article, 'In Memory of Alfredo Catalani,' was published in the Milan newspaper *La Perseveranza*. It is one of the best and most useful things ever written on the composer, and has been most unjustly ignored, as evidenced by the fact that over many years it has been repeatedly listed as published in September (even in the august *New Grove Dictionary of Opera*), whereas it was actually published between 6 and 9 August to mark the exact anniversary of Catalani's death. Nappi (1857–1932), a minor composer, was 'one of the most influential and authoritative Italian critics of the time.'[1] He had become the music critic of the *Perseveranza* in 1885, and also wrote for other newspapers and periodicals. He had met Catalani as early as 1875, and soon after became a friend, following the older man's career with a sympathetic personal and professional interest. In now choosing to publish some 'personal recollections' of the composer, along with 'information kindly supplied ... by his [Catalani's] friends and students,' Nappi was among the first to recognize that important biographical information concerning Catalani was in real danger of being lost.

Catalani often described himself as 'half lucky,' and this certainly applies to the matter of biography. Immediately after his death, his close friend Giuseppe Depanis had published a short biographical sketch of some forty pages: *Alfredo Catalani: Notes – Records (Alfredo Catalani: Appunti – Ricordi*, 1893; republished 1900). Depanis had almost no time for research, and relied largely on his own recollections, memories of what

---

1 Michael E. Henstock, *Fernando De Lucia: Son of Naples: 1860–1925* (London, 1990), 199.

Catalani had told him, and his large collection of letters from the composer, referred to above. His little pamphlet is absolutely invaluable for anyone seeking to find out about Catalani, but it is very far from a complete account of the composer's life. Unfortunately, it seems to have been just full enough to discourage anyone else from attempting a more extended biography. In 1903 it was valuably supplemented by Carlo Paladini's publication of some of Catalani's letters to Antonio Ghislanzoni and Ferdinando Fontana. However Paladini (1861–1922), a friend of both Catalani and Puccini who had published a serialised biography of the latter, disclaimed any responsibility for a more extended biographical account:

> I feel unable to write deeply and at length about Alfredo Catalani, nor would this be, for me, the right time to do so. But for this melancholy nightingale, too, the day will come for artistic popularity and the publication of biography; when musical taste will have become more refined, and audiences will not be hostile to, or forgetful of, the most delicate and inspired expressions of national art.[1]

Paladini felt that the letters would be 'of immense importance to the future biographer.'

By 1918 the situation prophesied by Paladini had, in part at least, come to pass, and in publishing his own 'recollections' Nappi was able to add very significantly to Depanis's account. He is the only source for many of the anecdotes he records. He was a good storyteller, and his article brings Catalani to life more vividly than almost anything else written on the

---

1 'Un Maestro di musica e due Poeti da teatro: Alcune lettere inedite di Alfredo Catalani,' *Musica e Musicisti* 58 (1903), 1041. For more on Paladini, see below, pp. 133–36.

composer. Nappi was a sincere admirer, but not a worshipper, and a friend, without being a member of the inner circle. His article thus achieves a skillful balance between sympathetic identification and critical objectivity. But there is real authority behind his judgments, and any admirer of Catalani will thrill at the high regard Nappi and other Italian critics had for the composer in 1918:

> We all believe that Catalani would have been able to create a wholly Italian music drama that would better respond to the exigencies of the music of today, and that would have dragged this musical genre away from the hybridity from which it has struggled to free itself for far too long.

Italian opera in 1918 was in bad shape: the promise of the 1890s had largely exhausted itself, no one had really emerged as 'the bearer of the Verdian standard,' and the international style that had taken over was unquestionably 'hybrid' – one just has to think of Puccini's diverse influences. Of course when artists die young it is always possible to speculate on what they *might* have achieved, and it is ultimately impossible to know where Catalani's obsessive search for a personal style would have taken him if he had lived longer. But Nappi the critic had been closely following the course of Italian opera since the 1870s, he was intimately acquainted with the issues of national style and musical modernism that all the younger composers had been struggling with, and his assessment of the latent possibilities in Catalani's work merits careful consideration.

One aim of Nappi's article seems to have been to encourage others to publish their recollections of Catalani, too, though in this he was not successful. The only substantial biographical account of Catalani to emerge in the following decade was written by Raffaello Barbiera, and included in his *Bathed in*

Glory and In the Shadows: Reflections and Recollections of the Nineteenth Century (*Nella Gloria e nell'Ombra: Immagini e Memorie dell' Ottocento*) of 1926. Barbiera (1851–1934) was an author, critic and journalist who spent most of his life in Milan, mixing in the city's fashionable literary and theatrical circles. It is not clear when he first met Catalani, but it was probably in the late 1870s, and almost certainly in the celebrated Milanese salon of the Countess Maffei, where Barbiera was a habitué. Barbiera's most successful book, *The Salon of the Countess Maffei* (*Il Salotto della Contessa Maffei*), first published in 1895, contained a brief and evocative glimpse of the composer in his early career:

> In the final period of the salon [which closed in 1886], there was a good deal of excellent music. Alfredo Catalani, wan and haggard, with a deathly pallor about his feverish face, played his supremely delicate music on the piano, dreamily longing for far away worlds and hidden paradises of love.[1] He reminded us of another young composer of prodigious talent, poor Adolfo Fumagalli, who was taken from us at only twenty-seven years of age![2] Antonio Bazzini, one of the salon's oldest friends, quite rightly beamed with fatherly pride whenever he heard Alfredo Catalani, undoubtedly his most outstanding student, play.[3]

---

1 In the original 'velati paradise d' amore.' This may be just a reference to the stock dreams of Romantic artists, but it is possibly a veiled allusion to Catalani's secret love affair with Teresa Junck, which Barbiera seems to have known about. See below, pp. 89–90.

2 Adolfo Fumagalli (1828–56), a virtuoso pianist and minor composer.

3 *Il Salotto della Contessa Maffei* (Milan, 1895), 306.

Later editions of this very popular book added a few details
about Catalani's music, and a remarkable claim that Catalani
had 'abandoned the idea of life in a convent, despite being attracted to it because of his yearning for solitary contemplation.'[1]
Barbiera is the earliest and possibly the only source for this bizarre biographical episode, which is considerably expanded in
the much fuller account of Catalani he reserved for his *Nella
Gloria* volume. Barbiera was no scholar or fact-checker, as several
mistakes in his account of the composer demonstrate, but in a
certain paradoxical way this authenticates his memoir: this is the
Catalani *he* remembered.

It is with Domenico Luigi Pardini that Catalani scholarship
can really be said to begin, and he attempted the first full critical biography (though his characteristic modesty prevented him
presenting it as such). Born in Lucca in 1864, Pardini lived in
the city all his life, dying there in 1951 at the age of 87.[2] As a
young man he studied at the Istituto Musicale Pacini, Lucca's
music school, where Catalani had been a student a decade
earlier. He subsequently became a primary school teacher, and
'rose up the ranks of academia' to eventually become the director
of primary education in the province of Lucca. Pardini was a
'historian at heart,' however, and devoted his spare time to local
cultural history, especially the history of music in Lucca. Given
his enthusiasms, it seems almost certain that he would have been
interested in Catalani from an early age. He nowhere suggests
that he actually knew the composer, but the account he gives of
Catalani being presented with a bronze crown in Lucca in 1892
strongly suggests that he was present:

---

1 *Il Salotto della Contessa Maffei* (Florence, 1915), 375. I am not sure in
which of the many editions of Barbiera's work this claim first appeared.

2 Biographical details are taken from the short, unsigned memoir of
Pardini published as an appendix to a reprinting of one of his articles in
Rassegna Lucchese New Series 19/20 (1984), 35.

Catalani grasped the rather modest crown presented by the Mayor between his frail hands,
as if clinging to it, and as his huge eyes, betraying all his physical pain and internal anguish,
turned toward the stalls and boxes, not overly
crowded, he seemed numbed by the applause.
He mustered the strength to utter the words
'thank you' with his pale and quivering lips. It
was an unforgettable scene![1]

It seems likely that Pardini was present, too, when Catalani was
finally buried in Lucca in March 1894.

In 1903 Pardini founded the periodical, *La Rassegna Lucchese*,
which he edited for many years. At this point, if not earlier,
his interest in Catalani became a publicly-declared fact. In the
January 1904 issue of *La Rassegna Lucchese* he reported Paladini's
recent publication of some of the letters, and commented:

Paladini says that he feels it inappropriate *to write
deeply and at length about Alfredo Catalani*, as he
believes the time is not right. Yet we would welcome what he has to say about Catalani, because
even though Depanis has written more than
anyone else about *this melancholy nightingale*,
and with the soul of a poet and all the affection
of a friend, he did not tell everything. Paladini
would be doing a great service to the history of
music, especially were he to give us a full account: one worthy of Catalani and the artistic
patrimony left to us by this noble musician.[2]

---

1 See below, p. 73. Pardini cites no source for his description, which
almost certainly proves this to be his eye-witness account.

2 This statement appears on the inside rear cover of the third issue of
volume 1, a space Pardini reserved for his 'Notices.'

Two years later, in the same journal, Pardini published a short and appreciative overview of Catalani's career and achievements, with considerable emphasis on the difficulties and injustices the composer had experienced.[1] This would become the germ of the later book.

Pardini was the sort of researcher who patiently collected materials over many years and, unlike today's academics, was in no hurry to see them in print. Thus it was not until the 1930s that he began to privately publish the fruits of what had obviously been decades of information gathering in a series of slim and unassuming volumes with the series title *Memories of Lucca* (*Quaderno di Ricordi Lucchesi*). The second of these, published in 1935, was devoted to Catalani. In some introductory comments Pardini made it clear that he did not want his book to be considered a 'complete' and critical biography – he hoped such a work would be written by someone else:

> A complete biography that tells of the salient vicissitudes of Catalani's life, that reveals the personal torment he suffered, his burning desire to work, and that includes precise analyses of his compositions, judging them with impartiality and diligence, has yet to be written. Yet perhaps we may not have to wait too long for a writer endowed with the ability and skill needed to fill this gap.

A footnote to this statement suggested that the writer in question was Carlo Gatti (1876–1965), Professor at the Milan Conservatory, who had published an essay on Catalani in 1918, as noted above. Gatti, who had briefly been a pupil of Catalani, was now famous as the author of a biography of Verdi (published 1931). His *Catalani: Life and Works* (*Catalani: La Vita e le Opere*)

---

1 'Alfredo Catalani,' *La Rassegna Lucchese* 3 (1906), 53–56.

would finally appear in 1953, but though it has some claims to be the standard biography, it is disappointing in many ways. It contains considerably less new information than might have been hoped, fails to digest a good deal of the information already published, and most vexatiously includes no documentation. It certainly did not make Pardini's humbler but more industrious efforts redundant – there is a good deal in Pardini that did not find its way into Gatti.

Pardini regarded his own book as less of a biography than a collection of materials from which a biography might be assembled: 'excerpts from documents, examinations, critiques and personal reminiscences.' He naturally regarded Depanis as his most important precursor in the field of Catalanian biography, and after Depanis seems to have considered Barbiera's account of the composer the most valuable (strangely, he shows no awareness of Nappi's article). Pardini's *Alfredo Catalani* is both primary and secondary source for anyone interested in the composer, or perhaps something in between. The first significant piece of Catalani scholarship, it was written with unique advantages. Pardini had breathed the same air as his subject and knew more about the Lucca where Catalani spent his formative years than any subsequent writer on the composer. If he did not know Catalani himself, he knew people who knew the composer, and he knew them when their memories were fresh. It seems clear that Pardini had seen manuscript materials that have since been lost, and his knowledge of the early critical reception of Catalani has probably never been surpassed: it is regrettable that he did not quote more generously. All this gives Pardini's biography freshness and immediacy, despite its 'documentary' style. Like all Pardini's books, it was printed in a small edition, and is very scarce today, only a tiny handful of libraries outside Italy holding copies. This 75th anniversary edition makes Pardini's researches widely available for the first time, and it is hoped that it will stimulate further interest in Catalani's life and work.

Pardini's *Alfredo Catalani* presents a reasonably full account of the composer, but it is only fair to draw attention to a significant omission and a significant misunderstanding. Pardini says virtually nothing about Catalani's relations with the opposite sex, merely remarking that women liked him, and hinting that an unnamed lady, who later donated a bronze bust of the composer to the Milan Conservatory, had fallen in love with him. It is probable that Pardini knew who this person was, but felt that the story was better suppressed. As the reader may naturally be curious about this aspect of the composer's biography, I have added an Appendix, 'Catalani's Loves,' to Pardini's account.

Pardini also seems to have misinterpreted Catalani's relationship with the powerful publisher, Giulio Ricordi, and indeed to have failed to grasp how the system of opera production worked in Catalani's period. Pardini names Ricordi as one who 'befriended and supported' Catalani, and he has 'the broad visioned and highly experienced publisher' enthusiastically buying *La Wally after* the opera had been produced. This, it might be noted, despite the fact that Barbiera, one of his main sources, had criticized Ricordi's treatment of Catalani. Catalani's letters from 1888 onwards are full of complaints about Ricordi, and with good reason.

Alan Mallach has recently emphasized how, in late 1800s Italy, 'publishers dictated which operas were to be performed and which singers and conductors would perform them.'[1] This meant the support of a publisher was absolutely crucial for any composer. Catalani was initially fortunate, being taken up by the aging publisher Giovannina Lucca (1814–94), who nurtured his career through his first three full-length operas, *Elda*, *Dejanice*, and *Edmea*. Unfortunately, in spring 1888 she retired, selling her business to her erstwhile rival, Ricordi, who thus acquired the

---

1 *The Autumn of Italian Opera: From Verismo to Modernism, 1890–1915* (Boston, 2007), 208.

rights to Catalani's operas. At this juncture Catalani's new opera, *Loreley*, was more or less ready to bring out; Ricordi, however, delayed promoting it for well over a year, so that it did not finally get staged until February 1890. A major reason was that he wanted to bring out Puccini's long-delayed *Edgar* (premiered April 1889) first, and even when Catalani's opera deservedly proved far more popular than Puccini's, Ricordi's clear preference for the younger composer was undiminished. Catalani was shaken by this lack of support, and dreamed of being able to break out of the system, writing of *La Wally*, which he composed without a contract, 'How happy I would be to be able to give this opera, without depending on any publishing house!'[1] But that was impossible, and though Catalani toyed with the idea of defecting to Ricordi's great rival, Edoardo Sonzogno, he did not do so, the main reason doubtless being that Ricordi would still hold the rights to all his earlier operas. Ricordi did show more enthusiasm for *La Wally*, which, contrary to Pardini's suggestion, he contracted to bring out well before the premiere. But he tied Catalani into an exploitative and unorthodox contract in which the composer would receive payment in three instalments, after the twentieth, fortieth, and sixtieth performances of the opera, and Catalani was also pledged to write his next opera for Ricordi. Even when *La Wally* proved very popular, Ricordi missed obvious opportunities to promote it, and ten months after the premiere Catalani wrote bitterly: 'Oh! "*rascal*" Ricordi! to think that I won't be able to get the sum set for *La Wally* until after the 60th performance, and we're only at the 38th!'[2] Catalani died before he could collect his final payment; given the distressing reports of his health and appearance in the final years of his life it is difficult to avoid the suspicion that Ricordi was calculating on this possibility.

---

1 Letter to Giuseppe Depanis, 1 January 1891. *Letters*, ed. Berrong, 83.

2 Letter to Giuseppe Depanis, 26 November 1892. Ibid, 123.

This introduction can conclude with brief mention of Catalani's subsequent reputation. The great upsurge of interest in his work that began around 1904 had largely exhausted itself by the late 1920s, though it is a remarkable fact that the first sound film of an Italian opera was *La Wally*, directed by Guido Brignone and released in 1932. In general, however, the 1930s and '40s saw a considerable slump in interest. The centenary of Catalani's birth in 1954 inspired a second revival. The 1950s was a golden decade for Catalani, with a number of publications (including three substantial biographies), several new productions, recordings, the emergence of Renata Tebaldi as the most celebrated interpreter of Wally, indeed of any Catalani role (she first sang the part in 1953), and even the appearance of a commemorative postage stamp with the composer's portrait. Nevertheless, interest gradually evaporated again, perhaps because of that aforementioned Mosco Carner effect, and since then Catalani has not held a place in the operatic firmament equivalent to that he occupied around the time of the First World War, or in the 1950s. *La Wally* is still revived reasonably often, and one aria from it – 'Ebben? Ne andrò lontana' – has become one of the most popular of all operatic extracts, regularly appearing in 'opera highlights' collections. But the other operas, though they have all (with the exception of *Elda*) been recorded, are very seldom staged. *Edmea* appears to have only been produced once since the Second World War (at Lucca in 1989). It is a delightful little opera that deserves better.

Lovers of Catalani can content themselves with Alan Mallach's recent conclusion that 'the beauty of his best music in *Loreley* and *La Wally* is such that he will never be entirely forgotten by the world of opera.'[1] But it would be better if this 'excellent musician,' this 'glorious yet unfortunate artist,' were remembered more often. And performed. And listened to.

---

1 Mallach, *Autumn of Italian Opera*, 57.

Further Reading

READERS WANTING to learn more about Catalani's musical style and achievement are referred in the first place to Jay Nicolaisen's excellent chapter on the composer in his *Italian Opera in Transition, 1871–1893* (Ann Arbor, 1980). Nicolaisen feels that Catalani was 'an extremely intelligent composer,' and that it is a 'tragedy' that 'Catalani's music is so little known … His last opera, *La Wally*, is so masterful a work and of such obvious stylistic importance that a scholarly examination of his entire oeuvre seems long overdue.'

Readers wanting to discover more about Italian opera and its context in Catalani's period, and immediately afterwards, are recommended to look at Alan Mallach's wonderfully comprehensive *The Autumn of Italian Opera: From Verismo to Modernism, 1890–1915* (Boston, 2007).

Readers wanting to learn more about Catalani himself can consult Richard M. Berrong's translation of his letters: *The Politics of Opera in Turn-of-the-Century Italy: As Seen Through the Letters of Alfredo Catalani* (Lampeter, 1992). The letters are not very remarkable as letters, but they do include many invaluable insights into Catalani's later career (there are only two from before 1880), and to a lesser extent his personal life. Berrong's annotations are excellent.

I intend to publish a translation of Giuseppe Depanis's writings on Catalani in the reasonably near future.

Note on the Texts

THE WRITINGS of Domenico Luigi Pardini, Giovanni Battista Nappi and Raffaello Barbiera translated here are essentially entire, and the slight cuts made in the main texts are clearly marked. Pardini was a compulsive writer of notes, and a few of his notes which have nothing to do with Catalani have been quietly omitted. His notes were originally published as endnotes, but to save the reader a lot of turning back and forth they are converted to footnotes in this edition. The only exceptions are the three very long notes given here as appendices. In cases where these writers referred to largely forgotten figures merely by family name, I have, where possible, added the Christian name to assist the reader.

The essays by Nappi and Barbiera were published without notes, so all the notes in this edition are editorial. Some notes added to Pardini's biography are marked 'ED.' Supplementary material added to Pardini's notes has been placed in square brackets.

Pardini's references have, where possible, been simplified and standardized. It has, unfortunately, proved completely impossible to check all his sources, and the reader must, to some extent, take them on trust. However an editorial decision has been made to reference Richard M. Berrong's edited translation of Catalani's letters wherever possible, even if Pardini was citing published extracts from the letters rather than the manuscript letters themselves. (Giuseppe Depanis had included extracts from some letters in his 1893 pamphlet on Catalani, but Pardini seems to have seen at least some of the original letters to Depanis, too, as well as other manuscript letters.) Pardini liked the 'op. cit.' style of citation, but for the most part that has been replaced here with either a full reference, or, in the case of frequently cited works, an abbreviated reference. A list of abbreviations used is given below.

Abbreviations

Alfredo Catalani. Beppino Lenzi, Aldo Berti and Nicola Laganà (eds.), *Alfredo Catalani: Nel Centocinquantesimo Anniversario della Nascita (1854–2004)* (Lucca, 2004).

Barbiera. Raffaello Barbiera, *Nella Gloria e nell' Ombra: Immagini e Memorie dell' Ottocento* (Milan, 1926). [A translation of the relevant section is included in the present volume.]

Cortopassi. Rinaldo Cortopassi, *Il Dramma di Alfredo Catalani* (Florence, 1954).

Depanis. Giuseppe Depanis, *Alfredo Catalani: Appunti – Ricordi* (Turin, 1893).

Gatti. Carlo Gatti, *Catalani: La Vita e le Opere* (Milan, 1953).

Letters. *The Politics of Opera in Turn-of-the-Century Italy: As Seen Through the Letters of Alfredo Catalani*, trans. and ed. Richard M. Berrong (Lampeter, 1992).

Nerici. Luigi Nerici, *Storia della Musica in Lucca* (Lucca, 1879).

Onoranze. *Onoranze al maestro Alfredo Catalani*, ed. Enrico Lippi (Lucca, 1900).

Schmidl. Carlo Schmidl. *Dizionario Universale dei Musicisti* (Milan, 1926). [A later edition of a work first published in 1888.]

Alfredo Catalani: Composer of Lucca

Domenico Luigi Pardini

[Originally published in 1935 as an 84-page softbound volume with the title *Alfredo Catalani: Quaderno di Ricordi Lucchesi.*]

'The harp hangs from the weeping willow, yet its strings ring true, plucked by fingers our eyes no longer see.'

— *Giovanni Pascoli*

I

ALFREDO CATALANI was born in Lucca on 19 June 1854.[1] His birth certificate tells us he was born in the parish of Santa Maria Corteorlandini and that he was given the forenames Giovanni Enrico Alfredo Felice. He was baptised in the church of San Frediano on 20 June.[2]

---

1 A few prefatory remarks are omitted here. Pardini mentions Lucca's glorious musical heritage and names Luigi Boccherini, Catalani and Puccini as the city's three greatest composers. He notes that though Boccherini and Puccini have been 'widely written about,' the same is not true for Catalani. He briefly reviews earlier writing on Catalani, then discusses the limitations of his own study. See Introduction, pp. 17–18. ED.

2 Pardini included a long note on Catalani's family and their living arrangements here. This is Appendix 1, 'Catalani's Family Background,' pp. 83–84. ED.

His father, Eugenio, was a music teacher who had studied with Giovanni Pacini, the composer of the opera *Saffo*.[1] He never enjoyed a distinguished reputation as a musician, yet he was much liked personally, and admired because of his gentlemanly ways and kind-heartedness. He taught privately and at the Regio Collegio. In 1850 he became an Associate of the Confraternity of Santa Cecilia, an association for which he composed his music, which was received with some favour.[2]

Catalani's mother, Giuseppina Picconi, was born in Cesena and after training as a teacher came to Lucca in the full bloom of youth as a tutor to the children of a noble family of the city. She married Eugenio Catalani when she was 28. She gave birth to three children: Roberto, Alfredo and Elisa.[3]

Giuseppina was an intelligent woman of noble sentiments. To contribute to domestic expenses she founded a girl's school where the abbot Matteo Trenta taught, in addition to other pedagogues of repute, including Pacini, Francesconi and Ghighizzola. She herself was an exemplary educator. Costantino Rossi,[4] who knew

---

1 Pacini (1796–1867) was a major opera composer who enjoyed great popularity in the 1810s and 20s; *Saffo* (1840) has always been regarded as his masterpiece. ED.

2 Nerici 76, 359, 372, 374. See further *La Provincia di Lucca*, 1883, which includes articles from *Il Pungolo di Milano*, *Il Progresso*, and *Il Fulmine Secondo*.

3 Eugenio Catalani (1825–83) married Giuseppina Picconi (died 1884) toward the end of 1850 (Alfredo Catalani 59). Pardini's claim that Giuseppina was 28 at the time of her marriage is contradicted by his own transcription of the parish records (p. 83 below), which suggests that she was the same age as her husband. The first son, Roberto, was born on 26 January 1852, and the daughter, Elisa, on 28 November 1858 (Alfredo Catalani 60, n. 73; 62). ED.

4 Costantino Rossi, born in Valenza in the province of Alessandria on 20 October 1832, was a distinguished and learned pedagogue. He was the Director of Studies at the Regia Scuola Normale of Lucca from 13 April 1882 to 1 March 1889. His published works were much acclaimed and served as handbooks for aspiring teachers. He died in Lucca on 4 January 1905.

Giuseppina well in a professional capacity, and was well placed to form an opinion, said of her: 'Endowed with a noble intelligence and uncommon culture, she is discerning, prudent, strict yet kind, measured in her praise, gentle when correcting her pupils, and always herself whatever the circumstances. She knows how to gain her pupils' affection, they think of her as a mother, and she earns the respect of parents who have complete confidence in entrusting their daughters' educations to her.'[1]

Despite her devotion to the school, Giuseppina never neglected the education of her own children, and in her they had the most virtuous mentor. Yet the threat of death hung over this household in which moral probity, productivity and the practice of faith were encouraged.

The first to die was the daughter, Elisa, and only a few years later followed the demise of Roberto, a promising and studious young boy gifted with a precocious talent for writing.[2]

One cannot imagine the pain and anxiety suffered by the young couple left with their only son, Alfredo, himself a sickly child, who was already carrying the terrible disease that had taken the lives of his siblings.

After her daughter's death, Giuseppina accepted the position of Headmistress at the Boarding School of the Regia Scuola Normale. Even today her work is remembered with profound respect, work that did not distract her from family obligations. Alfredo grew up in a loving household, yet his childhood was tinged with painful and melancholic memories of his siblings and a fear for the future. All this undoubtedly took its toll on his temperament.

---

1 See the booklet, *Giuseppina Catalani* (Lucca, 1884): '... an exceptionally fine woman of genteel appearance, mild manners, culture, integrity and a noble spirit who is universally admired.' See also *Il Fulmine Secondo*, 1884.

2 Regolo Nerici, *Alla cara memoria di Roberto Catalani* (Lucca, 1874). [Elisa died on 8 September 1871, at the age of 12; Roberto on 12 October 1874, at the age of 22 (Alfredo Catalani 65, 72). Both siblings died from tuberculosis. ED.]

While his father was privately educating him in music, Alfredo frequented the local state schools, where he was an able student. He was awarded high marks for his classical high school diploma, which he obtained from the Liceo Ginnasio Machiavelli in August 1871, demonstrating his natural aptitude for almost all his subjects.[1]

Some of Catalani's classmates, living today, remember him as a tidy, good-hearted and thoughtful lad, and a diligent student. Unlike some of the other boys, he was not particularly lively; in fact, he was often overcome with shyness and preferred to keep to himself.[2] During classes he would often dreamily write down musical phrases, and forget all about what was going on in the

---

1 He was awarded the following marks:

Written examinations: Italian 17/20, Latin 17/20, Ancient Greek 16/20, Mathematics 40/40, Philosophy 24/40.

Oral examinations: Italian 9/10, Latin 9/10, Ancient Greek 9/10, History 9/10, Mathematics 9/10, Physics 7/10 and Natural Sciences 9/10. (Records from the examining board.)

Catalani's classmates were the following:

Brugi Biagio, Cardella Domenico, Cherubini Giuseppe, Corvetti Giulio, Del Prete Ciro, Del Prete Guido, Del Re Adolfo, Favilla Acilio, Ferri Francesco, Filipperi Augusto, Francioni Giuseppe, Giammattei Giorgio, Giovannoni Angelo, Grotta Vincenzo, Lazzarini Giovanni, Lippi Giulio, Lucchesi Ascanio, Lucchesi Napoleone, Malenotti Gaetano, Massoni Luigi, Mugnani Felice, Pardocchi Ferruccio, Pierotti Ettore, Pierucci Fabio, Scarlini Giovanni, Silicani Pietro di Francesco.

Many of them became successful professionals; some went into teaching, others medicine, engineering and the law, some led distinguished careers in the civil service or wrote acclaimed literary and scientific works.

The handful of them who are alive today enjoy much deserved recognition.

2 A diligent classmate of his, Professor Fabio Pierucci, writes that 'Alfredo Catalani was a serious and studious fellow, and one of the top of the class. He was always sociable enough with his classmates, but I don't think he saw them outside school, because every time I saw him strolling around the city he was in the company of his father and mother, who I'd heard taught the piano.' (Letter to the author.)

classroom.[1] Perhaps developing in that gentle soul of his were the beguiling melodies that would lead to immortality!

Once Catalani had finished school his parents tried steering him toward a career as a lawyer or engineer, but the youngster was only interested in music, a subject with which he'd 'had a secret love affair at the classroom desk.'[2]

In the Catalani family a vocation for music had been passed down from father to son. Catalani's grandfather Domenico was a teacher and fine piano tuner. Felice, his uncle, was a pianist and composer of some repute, and his father Eugenio a skilful musician. This was a dynasty very much like others hailing from Lucca, the most notable being the Boccherini, Quilici and Puccini families.

The musical studies of the young Alfredo were entrusted to Fortunato Magi, a most able contrapuntalist, at the Istituto Musicale Pacini. He found in him a steady guardian who imparted a sense of self-assuredness, with an open intelligence that in no way compromised the natural disposition of his pupil but encouraged him to grasp with facility the rudiments of music. Catalani naturally profited from his teacher's knowledgeable instruction, so much so that at the conclusion of his course of studies, which lasted only a few months, he composed a Mass. His Sinfonia for

---

1 This habit of jotting down musical ideas was something that Catalani always kept up, even in his last years. The renowned violinist Adolfo Betti – who I will write more about in another book – wrote to me: 'I met Catalani also at Bagni di Lucca, when he was seriously ill. I remember him spending hours and hours in my father's pharmacy, slumped in an armchair, often mumbling out musical motifs which were then scribbled down in a notebook kept within hand's reach.'

He added: 'On one particular occasion he asked me to play him something, so I played Paganini's *Moto Perpetuo*. I recall him giving me some valuable tips on how to interpret the piece which had been given to him by Toscanini, who had recently asked all the first violins in his orchestra in Turin to play it.'

2 Depanis.

Orchestra and Romanza for Baritone were performed at the end
of the 1872 academic year prize-giving ceremony.

I shall give due consideration to these works later in the book.

In his studies with Magi the young Catalani learnt in depth
about the rules of composition. He had the good fortune of having a teacher gifted with a fine technique, refined taste and spirit,
and who kept up to date with the musical trends of the time.

It has been said that Catalani studied with Carlo Angeloni, yet
no official document exists attesting to this. Maestro Angeloni
was appointed Professor of Composition and Counterpoint in
1873, but by this time Catalani had already stopped frequenting
the Istituto Musicale Pacini.[1]

Prior to taking up this post Angeloni was in charge of other
classes, however. It is very likely that he may have given Catalani
the occasional lesson or some advice on a technical point; he
may even have looked over some of his schoolwork. The teachers
at the Istituto Pacini, especially in those days, were very much
like a family: they helped all pupils, and any sort of 'exclusive
rights' mentality was very much frowned upon when it came to
teaching any particular subject.

I myself have firsthand experience of this, having been a pupil
at the Istituto. I can testify to the exemplary friendliness and
esprit de corps enjoyed by the masters and students, this being
very much of benefit to everyone.

---

1 The fullest and most accurate account of Angeloni and his work is Luigi
Landucci, *Carlo Angeloni: Cronistoria* (Lucca, 1905). It makes no mention
of Catalani having been a student of this composer of so many popular
works. See also Domenico Luigi Pardini, *Carlo Angeloni: Quaderno di
Ricordi Lucchesi* (Lucca, 1934).

Documents exist attesting that Angeloni was appointed Professor of
Vocal Exercise and Bel Canto and a supply teacher of Organ Studies in
1862; that in 1864 he also taught the Theory and Practice of Harmony; and,
as already mentioned, that he was appointed Professor of Composition
and Counterpoint in 1873.

The historian interested in researching the musicians of Lucca cannot neglect the work of Fortunato Magi, who having been one of Michele Puccini's most promising students[1] was appointed Director and Professor of the prestigious Istituto Musicale Pacini. He brought a breath of fresh air to other similar institutions where he taught, his career culminating with the post of Artistic Director at the Benedetto Marcello Conservatory of Music in Venice. The following statement was made about this skilful teacher of harmony and counterpoint when he was still alive: 'This artist possesses all the qualities of a superb conductor, and he is an organist of superior musicianship.'[2]

The memory of a musician of such distinction, and his rich and artistically valuable compositions, simply must not fall into oblivion.[3]

Upon completion of his studies in Lucca, Catalani set off for Paris, where he studied at the Conservatoire; he was able to obtain a place without having to sit an entrance examination upon the presentation of his sacred work, his Mass. His piano studies were under the tuition of Antoine François Marmontel[4]

---

1 For Michele Puccini see Nerici and my *Carlo Angeloni* (cited in the previous note), p. 14, note 2. G. Pacini's pamphlet, *Ne' funerali di Michele Puccini maestro di musica* (Lucca, 1864), is well worth reading.

2 F. J. Fétis, *Biographie universelle des musiciens et bibliographie générale de la musique: Supplément et complément*, 2 vols. (Paris, 1878, 1881), 2:145.

3 See Appendix 2, 'Fortunato Magi: Catalani's Teacher,' pp. 85–86, for the fuller account of Magi that Pardini includes in a note here. ED.

4 Antoine François Marmontel, born in Clermont Ferrand in 1816, died in Paris in 1898. He studied the piano under Guillaume Zimmermann, whom he then succeeded, fugue with Jacques Fromental Halévy, and composition under Jean-François Le Sueur, all three of them first rate, renowned teachers. He left a legacy of studies, serenades etc., in addition to pedagogical works, including the well-regarded *Histoire du piano et de ses origins, influence de sa facture sur le style des compositieurs et virtuoses* (Italian translation by V. Morelli, 1904). Information from the *Biographie universelle des musicians*, cited above.

and his lessons in composition and counterpoint were with François Bazin.[1]

Competent judges have regarded Marmontel as a composer of little vitality: 'His works, albeit correct and elegant, are lacking in vigour and passion.'[2] Despite this some of his compositions are even today of didactic value. Although perhaps somewhat lacking in compositional talent, he made up for it as a fine performer and master of technique, as vehemently claimed by the many great pianists who graduated from the Conservatoire.[3] Catalani was a talented pianist who flourished under the tuition of his master, so much so that he could have carved out a successful career for himself as a concert pianist.

Catalani's musical culture was greatly enhanced by the erudite guidance of Bazin, who had much faith in his student, and who introduced him to many illustrious names in French music.[4]

Catalani pursued new musical forms and discovered uncharted territory, which he had not been able to do with his first

---

1 François Emmanuel Bazin (Marseille 1816–78) wrote several operas of short-lived popularity. He also wrote a rather good *Cours d'harmonie théorique et pratique*. He succeeded Ambroise Thomas as Professor of Composition at the Paris Conservatoire. There is a judicious account of him by Henri Blanchard in *Grand dictionnaire universel* 2:419. See also Andrea Della Corte and Guido M. Gatti, *Dizionario di Musica* (Turin, 1925).

[Pardini underestimated Bazin's importance as an opera composer. One of his operas, *Le voyage en Chine* (1865), was a major success, being regularly revived well into the twentieth century. Bazin was no innovator, but he wrote attractive, tuneful music and could have taught Catalani a great deal about the practicalities of writing for the theatre. ED.]

2 *Grand dictionnaire universel du XIXe siècle*, 17 vols. (Paris, 1865–90), 10:1229.

3 Here we remember the most famous: Bizet, Wieniawsky, Dubois, Planté, Diemer, Cohen and Thurner who were great concert pianists in France and throughout the world.

4 Here we remember, amongst others, the celebrated composers Charles Gounod and Georges Bizet.

teacher. This was all perfectly valid and legitimate, and through this voyage of discovery he refined his taste, without becoming overly dependent on French influences.[1]

Bazin was a great teacher of composition and counterpoint. His work was technically and harmonically impeccable, as was his instrumentation, yet it was lacking in imagination, originality and character. His operas were short-lived successes, nor did he enjoy any particular career highlights. Yet his lack of inspiration was compensated by his technical wizardry in harmony and counterpoint, and Catalani flourished under his tutorship. No works of Catalani's are held at the Paris Conservatoire, which he left in 1873, after his failure to make the shortlist for the Prix de Rome simply because he was not of French birth.[2] Immediately afterwards he moved to Milan, where he was admitted, again without having to sit an exam because of his having studied at the Paris Conservatoire, to the advanced course at the Conservatory.[3]

---

1 The Lucca newspaper *Il Figurinaio*, 1893, no.32, mentions the French influence in Catalani's music as a result of his Parisian education, though this was not in any way overwhelming, as can be evinced by a detailed comparison between Catalani's works and those of contemporary French composers.

2 I received this reply from the Conservatoire de Paris:
Monsieur,
I have received your letter of 30 January 1935. Despite lengthy research I have found no copies of Catalani's work at the Conservatoire de Paris. The Library does not hold any copies of his printed compositions or manuscripts.
      With sincerest regards,
            (Signature)

3 There is some uncertainty about dates here. Carlo Gatti later stated that Catalani returned to Italy in summer 1873 (28), entering the Milan Conservatory in November (33), while Rinaldo Cortopassi claimed that he did not return to Italy until March 1874 (49). Gatti's chronology, supported by Pardini, seems more likely; it is worth recalling that Gatti was closely connected with the Conservatory for most of his life and doubtless had access to records and oral traditions since lost. ED.

There he studied under Antonio Bazzini,[1] who could not have been a more suitable teacher.

The Milan Conservatory, having instituted a number of positive reforms, was at the time enjoying a better reputation than it had in the recent past.[2] The level of tuition was high, and Bazzini, who was known for the purity and expressiveness of his compositions, was particularly well regarded. His teaching methods were extremely efficacious, strongly attracting the students' interest, and guiding them in the beauties and rules of composition. He also taught classes in critical appreciation of works that were in vogue at the time, thereby encouraging knowledge and appreciation of the various schools of composition. Catalani benefited from this immensely, partly because Bazzini found in him a kindred spirit. Bazzini taught him with steadfast dedication, and he believed that the young composer had a promising future ahead of him.

Under the thoughtful and affectionate guidance of his three teachers, Magi, Bazin and Bazzini, all of whom recognised in him an outstanding talent and encouraged him in his aspirations, Catalani had equipped himself with a veritable treasure trove of knowledge. Yet he was not an ardent follower of any particular school, but simply followed his own instinct, and by doing so developed a very personal style. And his personality shone through when upon completion of his studies at the Milan Conservatory he presented as a final exhibition piece the opera *La Falce* (*The Scythe*).

---

1 Antonio Bazzini was born in Brescia in 1818 and died on 10 February 1897. In his youth he was one of the most fêted violinists of his time. In 1873 he was appointed teacher of composition at the Milan Conservatory, where he subsequently became Director. He was a prolific composer, his works much loved for their intrinsic value, style and powerful expressiveness. His most famous composition is 'La ridda dei folletti' ('Ronde des lutins').

2 The Director Alberto Mazzuccato, who had succeeded Lauro Rossi, was successful in giving the Conservatory a new lease of life. Schmidl.

II

AT THIS juncture we will examine some of the young Catalani's works, composed during his student years, between 1871 and 1875.

All musical geniuses, or those with a proven vocation for their art, have written music of some value in their youth. Such music gives an insight into the noble faculties of creativity. Catalani did not have a particularly precocious talent, but his early works, those composed when he was a student, reveal his brilliance and a very real affinity with his art. They represent the epitome of his character and, more importantly, his originality, a quality to be admired in all branches of the arts, and the single most important gift a composer can have.

Catalani was by no means a prolific student. His most notable student works, including those that were published and performed, are a Mazurka, Four Melodies for Voice, the Mass in E minor, a Sinfonia for Orchestra, a Romanza for Baritone, and his opera, *La Falce*.

The Mazurka and Four Melodies for Voice were published by the Florentine publishers Venturini; they were reviewed by the music critic Marquis F. D'Arcais,[1] who declared that the composer had been 'nourished by a fine education' and that his Four Melodies, *Il Sogno*, *Nella*, *La Speranza*, and *Il Morente* 'had an alluring quality about them, due to their originality.' He added that 'Catalani has his own ideas, and he is not an imitator of anyone else's style, which is a most worthy quality in a young composer in the early stages of his career.'[2]

---

1 The Marquis Francesco D'Arcais (1830–90) was a well-respected critic, writer and composer opposed to the direction modern music was taking. He was particularly opposed to Wagner's influence. [D'Arcais later infuriated Catalani with a negative review of *Lorely*. See below, p. 49. ED.]

2 See the 'Rassegna musicale' in the newspaper *L'Opinione*, 1872, and *La Provincia di Lucca*, 1872.

Catalani's Mass for Four Voices and Orchestra, which was premiered in Lucca Cathedral in May 1872, was a seminal work for the composer and received much enthusiastic praise for its wealth of melodies and harmonies. It was considered to be 'outstanding due to the clarity of ideas and original instrumentation.' Catalani had, with this work, proved to be a self-assured composer. Because it was very specifically a sacred composition, he concentrated on a careful elaboration of a strictly defined framework, a most fitting approach to this genre of music, which is unable to tolerate excessively sentimental melodies. Indeed, the Mass displays a certain austerity and empathy with the liturgical text. The fugues in the Gloria and Credo were particularly inspiring, as was the exquisitely written Agnus Dei with its religious sensitivity.[1]

The Mass was frequently performed, receiving the plaudits of audiences and critics alike, who praised it for its 'beauty, melodic qualities and spirituality.' Indeed it proved to be so popular that after its performance in Lucca Cathedral in 1900 it was the 'fervent desire of the citizens of Lucca' that there be a repeat performance.[2]

---

1 The Library of the Istituto Musicale Pacini holds an original copy of the Mass dated 28 March 1872.

An earlier manuscript of this Mass, described as 'a Quattro voci, con accompagnamento d'organo' and dated 16 February 1872, is owned by the heirs of the Maestro.

The Administrative Office of the Istituto Musicale Pacini has informed me that the Library holds other works of Catalani's, but that they are all secular.

The Libraries of the Paris and Milan Conservatories do not hold manuscripts of Catalani's sacred works. This Mass, therefore, is the only church music that was written by him.

2 For the work's performances and the critics' views refer to the following local papers: *Il Serchio*, 1872, *La Provincia di Lucca*, 1872 (which features opinions expressed in the *Gazzetta d'Italia*), *L'Eco d'Italia*, 1885, *L'Esare*, 1891, 1893 and 1900.

Although this work, when judged by the criteria of today, does not contain, as was claimed at the time, 'sparks of genius and an uncommon beauty,'[1] it does have its merits, and ones not easy for a young composer at the beginning of his career to master. It also proves that if the Maestro had focused on writing sacred music for the church his Muse would have distinguished herself, like those of so many of the fine composers of Lucca, who before the reforms instituted by Pope Pius X excelled with the jewels of their creation to the admiration and plaudits of many in the traditional religious congregations of Santa Croce and Santa Cecilia.[2]

On the strength of his Mass Catalani was successful in gaining a place at the Paris Conservatoire without having to sit an exam. This is a clear indication of the quality of the work, for Bazin was not easy to please, particularly in regard to a young, foreign student putting himself forward for a place on the advanced course at this world-famous institution.

No other examples of sacred works can be traced at the conservatories of Paris and Milan; indeed neither the original nor a copy of the Mass is stored in the archives of the Parisian institute, though as that was the work that secured Catalani a place at the Conservatoire it should have been kept.

As previously mentioned, Catalani had the Sinfonia for Orchestra and the Romanza for Baritone performed at the annual prize-giving ceremony at the end of the academic year 1872. Both works were very favourably received. It was written of the Sinfonia that it harmonised 'with sweetness and spontaneity,'

---

1 *Il Serchio*, 1872. The writer and politician, Giovanni Rosadi, a native of Lucca who should not be forgotten, regarded the Mass as 'a memorable work' ('Childhood Memories,' *La Nazione*, 1924).

2 Pope Pius X (1835–1914), Pope from 1903, issued a *motu proprio* in 1903 that recommended a restoration of older styles of ecclesiastical music, especially Gregorian chant. ED

that its quartet was a fine example of sophisticated musicianship, and that it was a vehicle for 'beautiful and melodious music' ably crafted to produce creative instrumental effects. The critic added: 'This young student must clearly have profoundly contemplated the work of Mozart.'[1] Note the use of the word *contemplated*, when it is easy enough for a novice composer to imitate a style, even with the inevitable differences that would occur.

The same critic, however, judged the Romanza less successful. The melodic phrasing was regarded as good, yet 'the accompaniment was a little too simple.'

Despite this, these student works were not lacking in a stylishness that hinted at the capabilities of a musician who had a long career ahead of him.

As has already been mentioned, we do not know if any of Catalani's works were performed while he attended the Paris Conservatoire. There is simply no evidence; yet perhaps one day someone may be able to shed some light on the subject, or may be able to research the archives of the institution in which the Maestro studied with such diligence, and with much success.[2]

We know Catalani's works were performed at the annual prize-giving ceremony at the Milan Conservatory,[3] yet the one work composed in his youth which more than any other displayed all his merits was his opera, *La Falce*, which he wrote as his graduation piece.[4]

---

1 *La Provincia di Lucca*, 1872.

2 Carlo Gatti went to Paris to investigate Catalani's time at the Conservatoire, but found no trace of him in the archives. He concluded that Catalani had audited classes rather than being a registered student (Gatti 25). ED.

3 An *Overture* by Catalani was played at the end-of-the-academic-year concert in 1874.

4 The original score is held at the Milan Conservatory, so the Administrative Office of this august institution informs me. It has been published by Ricordi.

It was performed in July 1875 in the theatre of the Conservatory as the composition he had submitted for his diploma.[1] It is worth remembering that Catalani was awarded the Special Prize for composition upon completion of his studies. He was a model student; earlier in the book there is an account of the success with which he had completed his high school education.

The libretto of *La Falce* was by Arrigo Boito (using the anagrammatic pseudonym Tobia Gorrio). His writing was highly original, and as a musician of substance to boot he was well aware of the limitations and the structure of the melodrama. He was an ideal collaborator for Catalani.

Regrettably, the work was under-rehearsed, and as a consequence it attracted widely varying criticism. Depanis wrote: 'To many it was a revelation, for others a scandal, for everyone an event. Anathema is what they hurled at the young artist of the future.'[2] But those who found it scandalous were not so much believers in progress as conservators of an art that, despite their personal antipathies, needed to move with the times. They were forgetting that even the great Italian masters of the 1800s, from Rossini to Verdi, had had to vent their creative genius. They had not, with blinkered determination, stuck to tradition: they explored innovative avenues and in doing so paved the way to new musical frontiers.

What the brilliant Giuseppe Mazzini had prophesied was coming about: 'When a school of thought, a trend, an epoch draws to a close, when you have put the seal to a lifetime's career and all that is left for you to do is re-live the past, that is when you are on the verge of reform, a reform that is inevitable and resolute because the powers of mankind cannot turn back.'[3]

---

1 Pardini mistakenly wrote August. *La Falce* was first performed on 19 July 1875. ED.

2 Depanis.

3 Giuseppe Mazzini, *Filosofia della musica* (1836).

Moreover, a much needed reform was being championed, the provisions of which had been written about as early as 1864 in the avant garde newspaper *Il Figaro*, founded by Emilio Praga and Arrigo Boito.

Catalani was a champion of change, but he was not the 'progressive' intent on provoking 'a scandal' that some critics, too set in their ways, made him out to be. Someone with foresight wrote of him: 'Our hopes for the future ride on this young musician. At twenty years of age he has yet to complete his course of studies at the Conservatory, and is already an absolute master of his art.' Of *La Falce*, he said 'it is a truly innovative masterpiece.' The orchestral writing is possibly finer than the vocal writing, and the music does not sufficiently cohere with the libretto, yet overall it is a display of exquisite quality. According to the well-respected critic Filippo Filippi, the prologue 'had a robustness and richly varied orchestral palette truly phenomenal for a composer at the beginning of his career.'[1]

The end result was most promising, despite the sometimes punctilious criticism it had attracted; and many were quick to defend *La Falce*. Indeed, an impartial critic interested in seeking out the truth wrote: 'We did not encounter the obscurity and avant garde inspiration we had been warned of. The music neither kills nor stifles the melodies that regularly burst clearly, and with impassioned spontaneity, from the soul of this young artist.'[2]

The critics were by no means disinterested. Those who reacted against the music were more often than not stuck in the old ways.

---

1 *La Perseveranza, Il Pungolo* and *La Provincia di Lucca* all republished reviews extracted from respected newspapers. See, too, *Il Fedele*, 1875. Filippo Filippi (1830–87) was a composer and distinguished music critic (Schmidl). [For more on Filippi, see below, p. 98 and note. ED.]

2 *Il Pungolo, La Provincia di Lucca*, 1875.

There was a desire for something new and original, yet when it appeared there was disapproval.

Catalani's triumph might have damaged many people's personal interests. It could also have relegated many works of the past to the dusty shelves of music libraries. And this youngster, who had just appeared on the scene, and who was regarded as 'a true master' with a promising future by the cognoscenti, ruffled many feathers.

The critic who discussed *La Falce* in the *Gazzetta di Milano* said well: 'In this work of a student there are many qualities all too often lacking in the writing of the older composers of today: originality, boldness, strength, and inspiration. Moreover, his writing displays the qualities we imagine those older composers having, such as erudition and faultless structure.'[1]

These were the words of the distinguished French critic and musician, Louis Ernest Reyer, who readily praised this first important work by Catalani, and drew attention to some of the best passages in the opera.[2]

So, in conclusion, *La Falce* was not the work of a fanatical follower of Wagner's music. A glance at the score today proves the groundlessness of the opinions expressed by those who waged a battle against innovation in art, either in a bid to protect their personal interests, or because of their technical ineptitude, or simply because of their lack of artistry.

Nevertheless, Catalani earned a reputation even amongst his adversaries as a profound connoisseur of musical beauty, and very few dared deny him his sincerity and originality, and his abilities as a skilful pursuer of musical effects.

---

1 *La Gazzetta di Milano*, 1875.

2 Ernest Reyer (1823–1909) was a composer himself as well as a powerful critic. He discussed *La Falce* with Catalani, and expressed the view that 'There isn't a single young man in France who could do as much!' Letters 71. ED.

III

ONCE HE had completed his studies at the Conservatory, Catalani set out to find gainful employment. His family was not in a position to help him very much, besides which, young and of honourable intentions, he was not keen to be supported, especially having earned a professional qualification.

He had made giant leaps under Marmontel, so much so that he had with much practice become a first-rate pianist, something which demands a mastery of a forbidding technique and superior powers of expression. Some of the friends he'd made in his musical circle encouraged him to give concerts, yet he was neither filled with a burning desire nor the strength to launch into a career as a concert pianist.[1] He had not yet been seriously afflicted by the hereditary disease that had robbed him of his siblings, yet he feared he might suffer the same fate. The recent loss of his brother Roberto gave him serious concerns. Running around the world giving concerts did not appeal to him in the slightest; in fact he preferred to stay in Milan, happy to live as well as possible by giving private lessons. The usual comforts of life were of little importance to him!

In the meantime Bazzini, who admired his student's kind-heartedness and warm nature, put in a good word for him with Giovannina Lucca, a music publisher of lively intellect who had greatly helped many artists.[2]

So Catalani continued earning his living by teaching, as well as composing short pieces, and getting to know influential people in artistic circles who admired his literary culture, vast knowledge of musical aesthetics, and integrity and eloquence when speaking about his art.[3]

---

1 For Nappi's views on this, see below, pp. 105–06. ED.

2 There is a profile of Giovannina Lucca in Schmidl (1:868).

3 At this period Catalani seems to have begun attending the famous artistic salon of the Countess Maffei. See Introduction, p. 14. ED.

He became known for his expert knowledge of the choral music of Italy and Europe, and in 1875 was appointed director and teacher at the Società del Quartetto di Milano, taking over from Martino Mhöder who had moved abroad. The newspaper *La Perseveranza* reported the news, describing Catalani as 'the young maestro who upon leaving the Conservatory caused such a stir with his short opera *La Falce*, a most original work.'[1] And this is how slowly but surely the Maestro's talent became known, spurring him on to continue in his work. He started looking around in earnest for a libretto that would unleash his creative energies.

It was in these years (1875–80) that Catalani wrote some memorable works which I've listed in no particular order: *L'Odalisque* for soprano, a *Barcarolle*, the *Chanson Groënlandaise* set to the words of Jules Verne, two works for string quartet, a *Scherzo*, a *Contemplazione*, and one or two other minor compositions.[2] They were performed with regularity and much admired for their musical merits by the cognoscenti, yet they were never to become popular as such. Catalani's reserve, dignity and quiet self-confidence meant that he never sought out 'any of that petty self-publicising so much favoured by the mediocre.'[3]

What Catalani did make sure of was that he was held in high esteem by the illustrious intellectuals of Milan. Those who befriended and supported him were, in addition to his teacher Bazzini, Carlo Pedrotti, Franco Faccio, Arrigo Boito, Giuseppe

---

1 *La Perseveranza*, 1875.

2 Various works are listed in the *Enciclopedia Italiana di Scienze, Lettere e Arti*, 36 vols. (Rome, 1929–37), 9:402. It is stated there that the *Chanson Groënlandaise* was incorporated into *La Wally*, becoming the famous romance 'Ebben? Ne andrò lontana.' And one of the string quartets, *A Sera*, was developed into the prelude to Act III of *La Wally*, a little gem which is often performed.

3 *Il Progresso*, 1880.

Depanis, Giulio Ricordi, Giovannina Lucca, the critic Ippolito Valletta and a host of other writers and musicians who championed all manifestations of the performing arts in the great Lombard city, all of which cast glory and lustre upon Italy.[1] Milan at the time was a centre of intellectual and artistic life.

Of the works mentioned above, the *Contemplazione* and *Scherzo* were performed at the Paris Trocadero in 1878 under the baton of Franco Faccio, and were most favourably received, despite the fact that the sheer size of the hall impacted somewhat negatively upon the acoustics and orchestral timbres.

The *Contemplazione* with its 'soft, sweet melody, a little reminiscent of Wagner' was judged, together with the *Scherzo*, as being irrefutable proof of the 'technical mastery' of the composer.[2]

But Catalani was worried about how he was going to make ends meet, and threw himself wholeheartedly into trying to find a libretto that would launch him on to bigger and better things. Yet he was beset by difficulties, clashes with others, and muted professional jealousy, all of which were to trouble him throughout his career, and which led him to state frequently, with some bitterness, 'I've only been half lucky.'

At this time Catalani was receiving a modest monthly stipend from the editor Giovannina Lucca, and spurred on by positive responses and encouragement from the music critic Ippolito Valletta had started putting pen to paper on his opera *Elda*, working closely with the poet Carlo D'Ormeville, who was

---

1 There is some confusion of dates and places in this list. Catalani only became acquainted with the conductor and composer Carlo Pedrotti (1817–93) and the critic Giuseppe Depanis (1853–1942) when he took *Elda* to Turin late in 1878; they were not part of the Milanese artistic scene. He seems to have had little, if anything, to do with Giulio Ricordi before 1888, when Ricordi took over Giovannina Lucca's publishing firm. It is not clear when Catalani first got to know the important composer and conductor Franco Faccio (1840–91), but a date in the late 1870s seems likely. ED.

2 *Il Progresso*, 1878.

preparing the libretto based on the Lorelei ballad by Heinrich Heine.[1] It was to have a legendary yet straightforward plot closely connected with the famous cliff on the banks of the Rhine where the 'fairest maid'

> ... *reclining*
> *In wondrous beauty* ...

entices the incautious helmsman to his death with her fatal and bewitching song:

> *He sees but the maiden before him,*
> *He sees not the reef or shoal!*[2]

Catalani was eager to get on with the task in hand, and the libretto suited his temperament. He worked on it arduously, with all the enthusiasm of his vivid imagination.

The innate artist was inspired by a mysterious and potent force which brought the images, sounds and inmost voices within him to life: he was pursued by his art much like a shadow. He became consumed by a feverish passion that drew him into his work with frenzied voracity to the exclusion of everything else; inspiration was at work, even in the midst of hardships, much like an invisible light penetrating a dull body.

On a bare canvas an artist sees the images he will have to paint, and in a shapeless mass of clay he catches sight of the statue his restless fingers will give shape to; in a similar way, the

---

1 For Carlo D'Ormeville (1842–1924) see Schmidl 1:460. [Pardini follows Barbiera in assuming that D'Ormeville developed the libretto from Heine's poem. This was not the case: *Elda* was adapted from Emanuel Geibel's libretto, *Die Loreley*, originally written for Mendelssohn, published in 1860, and subsequently set by Max Bruch. ED.]

2 *The Complete Poems of Heinrich Heine*, trans. Hal Draper (Boston, 1982), 76. Heine's untitled poem on the Lorelei legend had been published in his *Buch der Lieder* (1827). Pardini quoted an Italian translation by Tomaso Gnoli. ED.

songs restlessly stir the minds of both poet and musician until they become sublime words and notes entrusted to the paper anxiously grabbed to record them.

The terrible fever of creation, which consumes and obliterates almost all the day to day necessities of life; a fever that brings solitude and silence.

Catalani, at this time, was at the mercy of such an incurable fever, which allowed him no rest.

IV

BUT ENOUGH of this, let us talk about the works Catalani wrote in the second half of his career, between 1880 and 1893.

These were productive years, even though they were beset with conflicts and ill-health. It was during this period that Catalani saw performances of his operas *Elda* (1880), *Dejanice* (1883), *Edmea* (1886), *Loreley* (1890) and *La Wally* (1892), in addition to his symphonic poem of 1885, *Ero e Leandro*. This output testifies to the way he worked hard to achieve artistic truth, technical prowess, and emotional expressiveness, all of which he had consistently aspired to.[1]

---

1 The following works by Catalani are listed in the extensive catalogues of the Ricordi publishing house:

Chamber and Orchestral Music:

A Sera; *Serenatella*; Prelude to Act III of *La Wally*; *Ero e Leandro*, symphonic poem; *Contemplazione*; *In Sogno*.

Songs:

Chanson Groënlandaise; *Il m'amait tant* (romance); *In riva al mare* (barcarolle); *L'Odalisque* (chanson orientale); *Senza baci* (melodia).

Operas (with individual numbers and librettos):

Dejanice; *Edmea*; *La Falce*; *Loreley*; *La Wally*.

Piano Works:

A Sera; *Aspirazione*; *Contemplazione*; *Impressioni* (*Le rouet*, *In sogno!*, *A te*, *Sotto le tue finestre*, *In gondola*, *Canto di primavera*, *Rêverie*, *Un organetto suona per la via*, *Scherzo*, *Sans souci*); *Notturno*; *Ricordo di Lugano* (barcarolle); *Scherzo-tarantella*; *Se tu sapessi* (melodia).

For someone who was suffering from consumption and making ends meet by teaching privately and later at the Conservatory this was by no means an insignificant corpus of work. We can deduce from the dates that Catalani was writing consistently, and a look at the scores reveals a meticulous attention to detail, constant refinement, and exhausting workmanship. All this was achieved by a man who had a very brief life, full of trials and tribulations, internal struggles and spiritual crises; and who was weighed down by a far from happy domestic situation.

Just think what treasures Catalani could have composed with all that talent if he had been blessed with longevity and a calmer nature! It seems to be fated that those endowed with great creativity are more often than not condemned to a life of personal struggle and premature death. It is sufficient to recall Raphael, Giovanni Bellini, Giacomo Leopardi, Gaetano Donizetti, Torquato Tasso and Giovanni Battista Pergolesi, to name only Italians.

One of the factors delaying Catalani in his work was the lack of suitable librettos. He searched endlessly, saying: 'I've arrived at the point where I'd willingly commit myself to write an opera for nothing provided that I were given a fine libretto. Who will give me one? Who will give me one?'[1]

There was no shortage of librettos, but Catalani felt unable to accept them because he wanted to move away from the fantastic genre, which essentially suited his temperament down to the ground, because that sort of material no longer appealed to the critics. So he had to give up what he really liked, originality and personal expression, in order to conform to a different taste. Naturally he was dismayed at the prospect, and at times felt he no longer wanted to compose. 'I am ... tired of this artistic life of mine which still does not give me, either morally or materially,

---

1 Letter to Giuseppe Depanis, 20 January 1887. Letters 36. ED.

what it should be giving me!'[1] Yet his love for his art was such that he could not abandon it!

Catalani had clear ideas about the qualities he was looking for in a libretto, which would make it a success in the theatre, as he wrote to Antonio Ghislanzoni,[2] the writer in whom he confided often about his desire to work: 'Some maestros very much insist on the action taking place in one country rather than another, and make so-called *local colour* the principal issue. For me, all countries are good; not that I'm not concerned with the *colour*. Quite to the contrary! It takes a back seat for me, however. *Real, human passions*; this is what must be first! I don't even much like the characters in the libretto to be historical; I do, though, like the setting, the era in which the action takes place to be historical and known to the public.'[3]

He was given only a fraction of what he really wanted.

Catalani's works were widely discussed by critics, and even today are much studied. Naturally, they are not to everyone's taste, because not everyone has the same likes and dislikes, and what is fashionable and unfashionable plays a role, as do the artistic influences of the age.

If we were to relay everything that has been written by the critics on the technical and artistic attributes of Catalani we would have to compile a great tome consisting of a whole range of disparate opinions. Moreover, we would have to read such nonsense as that of one critic from Rome who dared write, claiming he'd heard a performance of *Loreley*, that 'It said nothing

---

1 Ibid. ED.

2 Antonio Ghislanzoni, a man of culture, most knowledgeable about music and a fine librettist, was born in Lecco in 1824 and died in Caprino Bergamasco in 1893. Schmidl 1:617. [Ghislanzoni, who supplied Catalani with the libretto for *Edmea*, is mainly remembered today as the librettist of Verdi's *Aida* (1871). ED.]

3 Letter to Ghislanzoni, 28 November 1883. Letters 9–10. ED.

new.'[1] This critic had probably never heard the opera, and it is most unlikely that he had even glanced at the manuscript.

We will briefly quote, in summary, some of the more authoritative reviews of Catalani's operas, written soon after the first performances, because we feel they are the most accurate and spontaneous, reflecting the taste of the time. We believe, too, that it is best to record the opinions of those who had a professional or critical duty to pronounce judgment when the works were first produced. Moreover, the emotions which influenced those judgments have their own importance, helping shed light on the truth. It is also interesting to compare and contrast the reviews of the past with those of today, because musical appreciation of today is very different from that of former times.

Elda turned out to be an exuberant work, like most musicians' first operas. Its composer had not yet learnt the secrets, the artifices, that ensure success, and he had let his fertile artistic imagination run riot. Catalani had found an impresario in Giuseppe Depanis's father,[2] which was quite an achievement, but shortly before the work was to be performed he was asked to make the opera brisker, to prune it down; so he took the advice of Carlo Pedrotti[3] and made the necessary changes and cuts,

---

1 Depanis. [The critic in question was Francesco d'Arcais, who had earlier praised Catalani's music: see above, p. 35. Catalani was incensed by his review of *Loreley*, writing to Giuseppe Depanis on 4 April 1890: 'I ask you to let me know if you know if the illustrious d'Arcais went to Turin to hear *Loreley*. If he did, he has every right to express whatever judgment, but if not (as I, positively, believe), I won't forgive him for the article in the *Nuova Antologia*, which would be real wickedness, to say nothing else. It must take a fine spirit to speak poorly of a work without having heard it, and to say that there's nothing "new!"' Letters 80. ED.]

2 Giovanni Depanis (1823–89), impresario of the Teatro Regio, Turin, from 1876. ED.

3 Pedrotti (1817–93), an important composer and conductor, was the director and conductor at the Teatro Regio. ED.

struggling with the internal conflicts, amounting to rebellions, that assail an artist when he has to make profound changes to his work.

Catalani wrote: 'Modifying is more difficult than creating, and one can never put too much time into the former.'[1] Yet this was an important lesson for him to learn for the future, because Pedrotti's advice, which was both valuable and sincere, proved to be most useful. If only that had been the only painful trial Catalani had to go through! The opera was performed under trying circumstances due to poorly rehearsed performers. Nevertheless, it was a triumph in Turin and even more so in Warsaw, where it was recorded that the success 'resulted from the intrinsic and patent value of the work, not from the fanciful whims of some benefactor or the indulgent passions of overly enthusiastic Italians.'[2] Yet the result did not please the composer, who felt that the music, always of the highest value, had been sacrificed to the libretto.

At the time Catalani was writing his new opera, *Dejanice*. He was determined to make a success of it, and to earn well from it, but he was to suffer a further blow. His father, whom he adored, died, and he felt that his family would never recover from this calamity.[3] He could not bear the thought of being apart from his mother, already afflicted with the pain of losing two of her children, so he decided to live with her, demonstrating his filial devotion. In a letter written from Lucca to the poet Ferdinando

---

1 Letter to Giuseppe Depanis, December 1878. Letters 1. ED.

2 *Il Mondo Artistico*, Milan 1881. *Il Fedele*, 1881. *Il Progresso*, 1880, includes some meaningful opinions expressed by Ippolito Valetta and Filippo Filippi. *La Provincia di Lucca*, 1880 and 1881. *La Falce* and *Elda* are mentioned in Torello del Carlo, *Storia Popolare di Lucca* (Lucca, 1880), p. 329.

3 Eugenio Catalani died on 6 November 1883, at the age of 58 (Alfredo Catalani 51). This was in fact several months after the premiere of *Dejanice* (17 March). ED.

Fontana[1] he said: 'I'm here to make the move to the capital. I've taken rooms in Milan [a four-roomed apartment], on via Cernaja, and now I'm sending the furniture there. My mother will come with me.'[2] But she was to live with him for the briefest of periods; just a few weeks later Giuseppina, the angel of the family, was to pass away.[3]

It is hard to imagine the pain Catalani must have felt at a time when he was so preoccupied with professional and personal challenges. He lost all enthusiasm for life, and in writing about what was being published about him and his work said 'Why should I care if the papers write about me? My mother can no longer read them.'[4] This kind-hearted, sensitive soul felt such grief!

Catalani had his mother's body brought to Lucca and buried her next to the family whom he had loved so dearly, then, broken-hearted, returned to Milan to continue his work.[5]

---

1 Ferdinando Fontana (1850–1919), a prolific and genteel poet who wrote many librettos, including Puccini's *Le Villi* and *Edgar*. With other illustrious intellectuals he was part of the Scapigliatura group in Milan. [The Scapigliatura ('dishevelled') movement started in Milan in the early 1860s. A literary, cultural, and political movement dedicated to the renewal of Italy, it opposed bourgeois values, classical standards in art, and parochialism. Catalani, too, was associated with the Scapigliatura. ED.]

2 Letter of 11 December 1883. Letters 11. ED.

3 Giuseppina Catalani died on 2 April 1884 in her son's apartment (Alfredo Catalani 53). ED.

4 *Il Progresso*, 1894.

5 This is how the kindly writer Maria Stefani-Barsanti recalled Catalani's distress at the death of his beloved mother, when her coffin was being taken to Lucca: 'Who can express in words the pangs felt by an ardent soul when death is close to him, love smiles upon him, art beckons him to greater things, and the whole world applauds him as, bathed in golden light, he sees before him new dreams, hears universal harmonies echoing deep within, and sees a crown of laurel descending upon his head? Who can express in words the battle between proximate, relentless death and elusive immortality?' (*Il Progresso*, 1894).

Dejanice, premiered in 1883 at La Scala, Milan, was a moderate success. Yet the critic Filippo Filippi, known for his uncompromising opinions, was full of admiration for the work. He said this of Act IV: 'The *Prelude*, which as a symphonic genre has gained so much in popularity with Wagner, is one of the most splendid pieces of orchestral writing I've ever heard. The writing is highly innovative, in terms of both its structure and instrumentation. It is also highly effective, which is most gratifying. The main motif in *F sharp minor* is truly inspiring, and beautifully framed by some very graceful passages full of pleasing harmony. It is altogether a most stylish piece of writing.'[1] The opera was then performed in Turin in 1884, and later in Nice in 1886. Although it was never to be regarded as a major work of Catalani's, it was valued for its moments of magic and passages of Bellini-like inspiration.

Revealed in this exceptional and masterfully written opera is the sure hand of a composer who exploited the resources of each instrument with indisputable skill.

Catalani wrote to Ghislanzoni just days before *Dejanice* was to be performed in Nice:[2] '... I've been living an unusual and troubled life here for the last twenty days. I've gone back and forth to Nice twice for the rehearsals of *Dejanice* (which had a really excellent success), I wore myself out, I even fell in love with a woman ... but I'll tell you the strange adventure in person; and with all that, God willing, my health continues to be fairly good, indeed better than what I would have dared hope. Now I'm here [in Milan] fighting the great battle, taking the decisive step in my artistic career.'[3]

---

1 *La Perseveranza* and *La Provincia di Lucca*, 1883. *Gazzetta Musicale*, Milan, 1883.

2 Pardini mistakenly wrote Turin instead of Nice. ED.

3 Undated letter of early 1886. Letters 24. For the mysterious reference to Catalani falling in love here, see below, pp. 92–93. ED.

A number of symphonic concerts were performed at the in-
auguration of the National Exposition held in Turin,[1] and the
Prelude to Act IV of *Dejanice* was performed in the second concert with great success. Margherita of Savoy was present, and she
'showed her obvious approval,' along with all the other members
of the audience.[2]

In 1885 Catalani's symphonic poem *Ero e Leandro* was performed at the Orchestrale Milanese festival.

This beautiful work made a deep impression on its audience.
The critic Giorgio Barini, writing about it in *La Tribuna* in 1906,
mentioned how enthusiastic the audience had been at that first
performance: 'And the applause,' he says, 'was amply justified.
Ero e Leandro is the work of a first class symphonist who knows
how to achieve superlative and meaningful results, rich in spontaneous and expressive melodies, to the extent that he has gained
the plaudits even of sceptics of that hybrid musical form, the
symphonic poem.'[3]

Next came *Edmea*, with Ghislanzoni providing the libretto.[4]
Again it was a success, and the critics wrote of its exquisite textures
fresh with inspiration, its melodic richness, Ulmo's Romanza,
Act II's impressive finale, and Oberto's Romanza. The finale of
Act II is a piece of truly skilful writing with sweeping statements,
imaginative colours, and evocative timbres. Act III also contains
some fine passages, the most notable being the gem of a duet,
'Tu sei qui – sul mio cor…,' the delicious sweetness of which

---

1 In April 1884. Giuseppe Depanis, Catalani's close friend, was actively
involved as a member of the Special Committee for Music. ED.

2 *La Provincia di Lucca*, 1884. It features reviews from other newspapers.

3 *La Tribuna*, 1906. Barini's article is entitled 'In attesa della *Loreley* al
Costanzi.' Giorgio Barini is a musician and critic of repute who has writ-
ten some good work. See Alberto De Angelis, *L'Italia Musicale d'Oggi*
(Rome, 1918).

4 *Edmea* was premiered on 27 February 1886 at La Scala. ED.

never failed to bring the house down.[1] The general opinion was that Catalani had made considerable progress in developing the structure of his operas, making them more truthful, and that the accusation of Wagnerianism was now without foundation. His music, with its singularly modern instrumentation, was melodically expressive in the best Italian tradition.

Edmea was widely performed in the opera houses of Italy, but for Catalani, as has been said, 'it doesn't constitute his true claim to fame.'[2]

The Maestro felt he had achieved something considerable, yet silence descended upon the opera, so he wrote 'It's a shame *Edmea* has to be lost! Couldn't we try to reacquire it again? If it is only a question of money, it would be worth the trouble to make some sacrifices.'[3]

Meanwhile, acting upon good authority, Catalani began revising *Elda*.[4] This opera, so rich in inspiration, which had revealed the composer's muse in a highly original manner, could surely not be destined for oblivion. The overriding problem was its poor and uninspiring libretto. In order for it to capture the imagination of the opera-going public parts of it needed

---

1 *La Voce della Verità*, 1888.

2 Depanis. *Edmea* was performed at the Teatro Apollo (1887), Rome's Teatro Argentina (1888) and Turin's Teatro Carignano (1889). *L'Esare*, 1887, 1888 and 1889.

3 Letter to Antonio Ghislanzoni, 28 November 1883. Letters 10. Pardini clearly misunderstood his notes here. At this date Catalani was simply concerned with obtaining rights to the libretto, which Ghislanzoni had offered to Salvatore Auteri-Manzocchi (1845–1924). ED.

4 The idea of revising *Elda* seems to have come mainly from Giuseppe Depanis. On 24 March 1886 Catalani wrote to him: 'Remember to send me *Elda* with the changes.' Letters 25. Depanis replied three days later with a long letter proposing an extensive series of changes that became the basis for the subsequent revision. See *Lettere di Alfredo Catalani e Giuseppe Depanis*, ed. Carlo Gatti (Milan, 1946), 28–30. ED.

a complete overhaul. It was simply too dry, and so the poets Carlo D'Ormeville and Angelo Zanardini set to work.[1] The result was *Loreley*.

Catalani confidently adapted the music, and said this of his latest exploits: 'It shall be my best work,' and he added: 'I'm ... convinced that *Loreley*, redone this way, will become a spirit worthy of respect, provided that she deigns to travel the world in search of "cash" for her papa.'[2] *Loreley* was completed in 1888. Yet not one opera house in the land opened its doors to the work, much to Catalani's despair.[3] He lived through two years of anguished suspense before the work was finally performed, and preparations and rehearsals for the event were far from plain sailing, as chronicled by Depanis in his highly readable book.

It was at this time that the music of Alberto Franchetti, Giacomo Puccini, Pietro Mascagni and Ruggiero Leoncavallo was enjoying much popularity, all of which was of no help to Catalani. He was to remark bitterly: 'Lucky them, that have been able to hit the nail on the head; I certainly haven't!'[4]

---

1 Angelo Zanardini (1820–93) was a composer and eminent librettist. It was he who wrote the libretto for *Dejanice*. Luigi Illica was also involved in the re-writing of *Elda*, which then became *Loreley*.

2 Letter to Giuseppe Depanis, 2 January 1887. Letters 35. ED.

3 The delay in getting *Loreley* produced was essentially the result of inaction on the part of Giulio Ricordi, Catalani's new publisher, however. See Introduction, pp. 19–20. ED.

4 This statement comes from a letter to Giuseppe Depanis of 28 February 1893, but had been adapted by Depanis in his 1893 pamphlet on Catalani; Pardini quotes the adapted version. Catalani had referred simply to Puccini: 'Beato lui, che ha ...' (Lucky him, that has ...). See *Lettere di Alfredo Catalani e Giuseppe Depanis*, ed. Carlo Gatti (Milan, 1946), 154. Depanis changed this to 'Beati loro, che hanno ...' (Lucky them, that have ...) and made it refer to Mascagni and Leoncavallo as well (Depanis 18), which was doubtless faithful to Catalani's feelings. Richard M. Berrong translates, a little oddly, 'Lucky him, who has known how to run into debt ...' Letters 129–30. ED.

The first production of *Loreley* was a satisfying success, yet there was some unfavourable criticism.[1] However, it was an altogether more lithe and better proportioned work, and it demonstrated the composer's technical mastery.

Loreley was performed on alternate evenings with *Lohengrin*; and owing precious little to Wagnerian music it stood out because of its own style. It combined 'the modern with a more traditional compositional style, with all the consummate finish of Italian convention, and satisfied even the most fastidious opera lovers.'[2] It was widely written about in the press, the critics most judiciously observing that the composer of the score demonstrated 'a lofty high-mindedness and education in the most exacting musical disciplines.'[3] They praised the qualities of the work, though there were those who remarked defects, despite commenting positively on the musical variety and richness of its score, noting in particular the delicious aria in Act II, 'Vieni al mio sen, stringimi al cor,' the Dance of the Ondines, and the refinement and tenderness of Act III. The orchestral writing was held to be 'well conceived and felicitous,' others thought the composer 'a little too self-assured in his creative powers, but primarily most honest.'[4] And honesty in art is a gift of paramount importance.

The opera went the rounds,[5] and despite the occasional

---

1 *Loreley* opened at the Teatro Regio, Turin, on 16 February 1890. ED.

2 *L'Esare*, 1890. *Il Fracassa* and *Il Figurinaio*.

3 *L'Esare*, 1890.

4 *Il Figurinaio*, 1893. Attilio Luzzatti wrote of Catalani's capable musicianship and honesty of character in the highly reputable broadsheet *La Tribuna*. A most laudable trait at a time of unscrupulous commercialism and claques!

5 *Loreley* was performed to much critical acclaim in, amongst other cities, Genoa, Turin and Rome. The performances in Rome inspired, as was written at the time, 'a truly profound fascination at a time when dozens of new works by young Italian and foreign composers are falling by the wayside' (*Il Progresso*, 1893).

criticism, which one must expect with all human endeavours, Catalani was finally hailed as one of Italy's finest composers, and 'the most noble and refined of all.'[1] And that was no exaggeration!

There were other stars, already mentioned, that were bright sparks in the constellation. Puccini, Mascagni and Leoncavallo all had their fair share of success with great works which better caught the imagination of the opera-going public. Yet despite this, Catalani's work was never underrated by the cognoscenti, who valued the fact that his was the writing of a man both learned and original, who with utmost integrity pursued his artistic mission, and who was not prepared to make compromises in order to curry favour with the public and critics, which he felt would have been dishonest.

What was still not up to scratch, despite the abilities of at least one of the writers, was the libretto. It is only right that at this juncture we quote Raffaello Barbiera's opinion: 'I simply do not know how Catalani was able to clothe such an abomination in beautiful melodies worthy of the true legend of the Lorelei of the Rhine; melodies which, unlike the songs of the temptress, save and elevate the opera.'[2]

It is unfortunately fair to say that many operas have been let down by substandard librettos, and for this reason they have fallen by the wayside. Swathes of beautiful music have been relegated to many a dusty library shelf.

We are now nearing the end of Catalani's life. He had for two years taught at the Milan Conservatory,[3] having taken over from the distinguished composer Amilcare Ponchielli, and he was still searching high and low for a libretto that would suit his artistic

---

1 *Il Figurinaio*, 1893.

2 Barbiera.

3 After a long delay caused by doubts about his health, Catalani had taken up his teaching position at the Milan Conservatory in April 1888. ED.

temperament yet also take him away from the fantastic genre which had previously been his preferred choice.[1] While Luigi Illica[2] was working on *La Wally*, the Wagner cult, which had steadily developed since 1878, reached the peak of idolatrous enthusiasm. Neither men of stature, nor honourable strides taken forward in the arts were respected. Even the great Verdi was a target for criticism. Severe comments were levelled at Catalani, 'accused of Wagnerian mannerisms at a time when Wagner was regarded as a musical antichrist, and all of a sudden accused of lese-majesty when Wagner was the Word and completely infallible.'[3] Criticisms are, as has always been the case, hurled hard and fast at those who are bravely innovative, and those who have risen above mediocrity.

Catalani was hurt by this unjust and malevolent criticism, writing: 'I'm living … like a patient snail, which for the moment

---

1 Here is a list of just a few of the librettos Catalani either considered or tried to obtain: *Lo Schiavo* from the novel by Demidoff, *Onesta*, *Francesca*, *Sotto la Reggenza* and *Teodora*. The papers wrote about Catalani's interest in *Teodora* and the composer wrote to Ghislanzoni: 'Don't deny the news, because that's what, in fact, should happen. I was struck by that drama, and I want to set it to music.' [Letter of 17 December 1885. Letters 21.] Others that had attracted his attention were Pietro Loti's *Pêcheur d'Islande*, André Theuriet's *Canonichessa* and Luigi Illica's *Rusalka*. Depanis.

Catalani discarded the play *Sotto la Reggenza* because of its similarity to Verdi's *Rigoletto*.

[Of all these possible subjects, it seems to have been Loti's *Pêcheur d'Islande* that Catalani was most seriously interested in: see below, pp. 134–35. It is worth pointing out that of all Catalani's operas only *Elda* and *Loreley* can in any sense be said to belong to the 'fantastic genre.' ED.]

2 Luigi Illica (1857–1919) was a prolific and highly regarded journalist and man of letters who wrote many greatly admired librettos (Schmidl 1:737). The libretto for *La Wally* was adapted from the novel by Wilhelmine von Hillern. [*Die Geier-Wally. Eine Geschichte aus den Tyroler Alpen* was published in German in 1875; an Italian translation was serialised in 1887. See below, pp. 118–20. ED.]

3 Depanis.

has his horns drawn in, ready to stick them out at the first opportunity; and then, I hope, they will have become horns so hard and so long that they will pierce at least a couple of critics.'[1] But this artist's star had always been crossed by clouds. Not only was he perturbed by comments made about his Wagnerianism, he was also plagued by veiled or obvious antipathies, jealousy, and fusses made over the work of inexperienced composers, in addition to well orchestrated attacks aimed at diminishing and belittling his talents and fame.

His health, both physical and mental, suffered as a consequence, and he had bouts of depression and self-doubt which drew him to mysticism. It was when he was working on *La Wally* that he retreated to a convent, and this together with other events can be read about in Raffaello Barbiera's book. I cannot go into them here for the sake of brevity.[2]

After some considerable time *La Wally* was ready, and it was welcomed with ebullient enthusiasm by the publisher Giovannina Lucca: 'It's been so well written, I'm sure of its success, and the comfort it will give its unhappy composer' who perhaps *is counting his last days*.[3] Might Catalani have heard those painful words? He was now very ill, despite his noble attempts to keep body and soul intact, and the prospect of death was looming large.

The 1892 premiere was nothing short of an unmitigated triumph. The broadsheet *Il Corriere della Sera* wrote that this new

---

1 Letter to Giuseppe Depanis, 3 August 1890. Letters 81. ED.

2 Barbiera. [A reference to one of the most mysterious episodes in Catalani's biography. For Barbiera's account and the problems it raises see below, pp. 128–129. It is unfortunately unclear whether Pardini accepted the convent story solely on Barbiera's authority, or had other reasons for believing it. ED.]

3 Ibid. [Pardini paraphrases Lucca's speech, made at a rehearsal for *La Wally*. For Barbiera's memory of it, see below, pp. 129–30. ED.]

opera 'was a highly personal work,' not in the least bit 'vulgar, unlike so many other operas' being performed with regularity.[1] The critics were unanimous in their praise, writing in detail about the beauty of the music, and Verdi himself, having attended the seventeenth performance, 'declared his real enthusiasm.'[2] It was a known fact that the great Maestro was always honest in his opinions, and by making such a declaration he was vouching for his esteem of the composer. The broad visioned and highly experienced publisher Giulio Ricordi, having attended a performance, purchased the opera because it was 'fast-moving, interesting, vigorous, and full of youth.'[3]

It could not have been better received!

Other productions of *La Wally* followed, both in Italy and abroad, and with much success. Catalani had honed his skills over many long and arduous years of study; his music was refined and majestic, and what prevailed was a sense of humanity and truth which touched audiences' hearts and inspired admiration. The opera's melodic lines, clarity, spontaneity and elegance are sustained by finely wrought, perfect instrumentation. The music is beautifully tied to what takes place on the stage, is skilfully coloured, and allows the singers to exude a beguiling passion, most notably in the gem of an aria 'Ebben? Ne andrò lontana.'[4] All these qualities contribute to making this score of Catalani's his chef-d'œuvre, a work which will forever give consolation to

---

1 *Corriere della Sera*, 1892. For other reviews of the opera see *Il Figurinaio* and *L'Esare*, 1892.

2 *Il Telegrafo*, 1892. The opera received 18 performances in Milan.

3 This report of Ricordi's opinion comes from a letter Catalani wrote to Giuseppe Depanis on 24 June 1891 – that is, some six months before the opera's premiere (Letters 88). As discussed in my introduction, Pardini was clearly confused about the relationship between Catalani and Ricordi. ED.

4 *Il Figurinaio*, and an important review featured in *Secolo XIX*, 1892.

the soul, that reveals the beauty of artistic creation and the most intimate sentiments of its composer.[1]

With *La Wally* Catalani made a name for himself as a thoroughly modern composer of operas, so much so that he was regarded as the leader of a new Tuscan School which certainly owed little to Wagner.[2]

It would be appropriate at this juncture to give a precise technical overview of Catalani's work, but it would be an arduous task requiring infinitesimal and painstaking attention to detail, which I regrettably feel incapable of undertaking. Perhaps it would be wiser for someone who has a more profound knowledge of music to attempt this. What I can say is that the qualities of spontaneity, grace, refinement and technical mastery are all prominent in Catalani's music.

It can be observed that Catalani's choice of minor keys lends a melancholic air to his music: and it is said that he wrote this way because of his poor state of health. This may well be the case, but an artist must enquire of himself concerning the best that his temperament can provide, because failing that his music can become contrived and false. How many composers have failed to follow their instinct, producing instead works that are far removed from reality, lifeless, and of short-lived glory?

---

1 See some important reviews of Catalani's work in the various volumes of the *Gazzetta Musicale* from 1880 onwards.

2 In a letter of 1900 Depanis revised his earlier opinion that Catalani, Puccini and Mascagni had formed a 'Tuscan School,' perhaps because of certain similarities shared by *Le Villi* and *Elda*, *Le Villi* and *Cavalleria Rusticana*, and *Manon* and *La Wally*. What he subsequently thought was that: 'Catalani is the leader of the Italian *giovane scuola* ['young school'].' This is certainly more accurate and justifiable. Adolfo Betti wrote: 'It is absolutely right to think that certain passages of Puccini's music (and I refer in particular to *Manon*) would not have been written, or would have been very different, had it not been for the works of Catalani that preceded them.' *Onoranze al maestro Alfredo Catalani* (Pescia, 1932). [Depanis's 1900 letter was published in Onoranze, 23–24. ED.]

Catalani's melancholic muse is not oppressive, nor does she dishearten her audience. She moves her listeners, and when the feelings run deep she brings us to tears, without, however, leaving us with a lingering trace of anguish. This is true art, and when it comes to the sentiments of love and nature our Catalani was a genuine master.

It is said that while Catalani was developing as an artist he was very much influenced by Chopin, Bellini, Bach, Mozart, and most significantly Wagner.

Many composers, even the most original, have at some stage in their careers been touched and influenced by predecessors in whom they find a kindred spirit.

According to Verdi, Rossini had appropriated 'something of Mozart's style,' and hints of Spontini, Auber and Meyerbeer can be discerned in Wagner's earlier operas. Barbiera asserted, and we could not possibly argue, that Puccini was very much taken with 'certain characteristics' of Catalani, 'and they influenced him.'[1] What is crucially important is that composers do not imitate one another, and do not stick doggedly to one school and a particular format. What they must do is develop their own individual style and personality, and personality, as Catalani once said, 'should speak for itself.' Yet inevitably certain traits are common amongst those handling pen, paintbrush and manuscript paper.

Today, accusations that Catalani's music is Wagnerian have largely been abandoned. Catalani's musical concepts and what they stand for are quite different, and very distant from Wagnerian ideals. All we need do to prove this is to examine what has been written, without preconceived ideas, by those who have analysed and scrutinised Wagner's innovative and powerful work in detail, and found it totally personal to him.

In his thoughtful and beautifully written study, well worth reading, Carlo Giuliozzi writes: 'All Wagner's music is essentially

---

1 Barbiera.

symbolic, both in a dramatic and musical sense.' He goes on to say: '... it is worth recognising that Wagnerian music is the ultimate demonstration of the art without grace.'[1]

Catalani's music does not contain the artifice so favoured by the great German composer. He is modern in his instrumentation, yet at the same time adheres to Italian traditions. The sentiments of love, joy and sorrow are expressed in graceful, polished arias which console and move the listener. There is no danger of Catalani's works sharing anything with the sort of false art, unfortunately now very fashionable, prophesied by the immortal Rossini.[2]

The foundations of Catalani's works were succinctly summarised by the composer himself as follows: 'What is of utmost importance is the inherent expressiveness of what is in the drama, something words cannot describe nor define, not the acoustic and instrumental accompaniment of the words of an opera.'[3]

And we are not claiming that Catalani was unduly influenced by the 'musical traditions of France, for which, in any case, he should have instinctively felt an affinity. No, he was more influenced by lasting memories of his early studies and the intimate sentiments of his temperament.'[4]

An impartial analysis of Catalani's work to seek out the truth reveals him to be a most original and refined composer, whose music, rich in colour, is in keeping with the finest traditions of composition, boasting all the beauty and passion of a sensitive and well-intentioned soul.

---

1 *Riccardo Wagner. La sua opera e la sua utopia* (Milan, 1910).

2 Rossini wrote in a letter to Luigi Ferrucci: 'The head shall win over the heart, science shall overturn art, and men's voices and feelings shall be buried under a shower of notes issuing from instruments.'

3 Pardini gives no reference for this interesting statement, but it comes from a letter to Stefano Stampa (the stepson of Alessandro Manzoni): see Michelangelo Zurletti, *Catalani* (Turin, 1982), 36. ED.

4 *Il Figurinaio*, 1893.

Many are the gems that can be counted in Catalani's music. The instrumentation is always done skilfully.

Catalani's chorus writing is without question superlative. Examples include the chattering throngs in *Edmea*, the courtesans in *Dejanice*, the elderly women in *Loreley*, and the hunters in *La Wally*. Not only do these choral pieces display a purity of style, they are most thoughtfully written and rich in harmonic content. The dances are also highly original, and the descriptive passages ebb and flow and develop beautifully.

There are, regrettably, the occasional shortcomings in Catalani's music, and some are quite glaring. But is it possible for a human being to write the perfect opera?

At this point we should agree that these failings cannot adversely impinge upon the stature of our composer, who unstintingly endeavoured to improve himself, taking into serious consideration what his critics said of him, in addition to the opinions of opera-going audiences, and the trends of the time. All this led to him touching the truth, which in expressions of art is the basis of beauty, eternity and glory. And when he applied himself, he succeeded.

Yet Catalani's untimely death deprived us of the definitive work of his genius, sensibility, and technical virtuosity.

I take pleasure in concluding with the opinion expressed by a most honourable and impartial critic: 'Alfredo Catalani ignored spasmodic ravings, violent outbursts, and the heat and impetus of intoxicating passions. He adored purity and sweetness, elegant gracefulness, exquisite refinement, and sentimental melancholy.'[1]

---

1 Arnaldo Bonaventura, 'Commemorazione' in Onoranze. [Bonaventura is clearly suggesting that Catalani distanced himself from the 'ravings' and violence of the 'verismo' style. ED.] Although G. A. Biaggi was not a great champion of Catalani's work, he did write the following: 'His style reveals an exemplary purity and nobility. His intentions are always high-minded and poetic.' *Nuova Antologia*, 1926, 3rd series, 7th number.

V

Catalani's economic situation was inadequate for his needs, and he had inherited very little from his family. His private lessons, operas and other professional commitments were far from lucrative, and he wore himself out, particularly when writing his music.

Amilcare Ponchielli died in 1886 and the post of Professor of Composition at the Milan Conservatory became vacant.

Catalani's friends and admirers, all of whom loved him dearly and wished him a life of greater peace and security, urged him to apply for the post. This advice was given, too, because it was widely believed that this important academic position, held by an eminent composer of vast and sound culture, and uncompromising enthusiasm, would be of advantage to all concerned, and of benefit to the future art of music.

Although Catalani had no great aptitude for life in academia, he was aware that he needed a regular income, and this spurred him to seek permanent employment. He knew the profits he earned for his efforts and his works were rather meagre and sporadic, and that the excessive daily strain was damaging to his health.

What he really wanted was to give up teaching so that he could throw himself wholeheartedly into his operas!

Catalani's letters to Alfredo Caselli, Giuseppe Depanis and Arturo Toscanini all reveal his underlying, noble sentiments, and the firm, steady temperament of a man living for his art, prepared to make sacrifices and live modestly:[1] but this utopian vision, an artist's dream, did not coincide with the reality of day-to-day life. Past experiences had taught Catalani to live life cautiously.

---

1 Catalani corresponded with Alfredo Caselli, a businessman and journalist and friend of many illustrious writers and musicians. A plaque commemorating his life has been placed on his house in Piazza Guidiccioni.

Applications for the post of Professor of Composition at the Milan Conservatory were invited on two occasions, with no appointment being made. Catalani decided to submit his application on the third occasion, and was successfully chosen for the post by the selection panel, yet his physical health was called into question, so the official appointment was delayed. The authorities expressed their fears that Catalani might not have the physical strength to cope with the demands of this important academic post, and there was some opposition from competitors determined to undermine his position. All this made Catalani restless. He did not like people talking about his health, and said: 'I would be the first to resign if I saw that my health was causing a problem. I wouldn't be at all surprised if my opponents managed to persuade the Minister that I'm a poor consumptive at the last stages [of his illness]. I would regret far more not getting the post for this reason than if they proved that I was an ass. At least I could prove that I'm not an ass!'[1]

Just imagine how this poor man, with his great sensitivity, was condemned to such bitterness! He spoke of his unhappiness in this way: 'Oh! what a comedy the world is, and what an ugly comedy! And how tired I am of it.'[2] More precisely, he was tired of the tragedy of life, which made him feel that he was forever shadowed by the spectre of death. So he hung on dearly to life with fiery passion, inspired by his ideals, which he was unable to fulfil without anguish. Catalani's agony was

---

1 Pardini gives no reference here, but quotes from letters to Giuseppe Depanis of 28 and 31 March 1888. Letters 50. ED.

2 Letter to Giuseppe Depanis, 20 August 1889. Letters 65. The remark was actually prompted by the recognition that Ricordi openly favoured Puccini, and the belief that Verdi himself was pulling strings on behalf of the latter's *Edgar*: 'now there are "dynasties," even in art, and I know that Puccini "must" be Verdi's successor…' Catalani had been waiting a long time to see *Loreley* staged, and the letter reflects a much deeper disillusion than any of his earlier letters to Depanis. ED.

captured by the artist Tranquillo Cremona in his well-known painting *L'Edera* ('The Ivy'), which clearly represents the sad and dreadful truth![1]

After some discussion the position was finally assigned to Catalani,[2] and he threw himself into his work with exemplary diligence. He taught with the utmost conscientious skill, instructing his students in the finer points of the techniques of composition. He adored his students, and would say: 'A curse upon him who dares malign them!' He followed them closely, encouraging enthusiasm, passion and individual preferences, and affirming: 'if a student of mine feels that way [i.e. wants to compose in a modern style], why should I have to turn him aside? In music, all genres are good, provided that they're felt and well done.'[3] How fair and wise.

Catalani was like an older brother to his pupils. Many remember the time when, in order to showcase the talents of one particular student, 'he informed everyone that he did not want to have one of his own pieces performed.'[4] This was indeed a very rare move! Many distinguished students were under his tutorship, and all of them admired him immensely. His students

---

1 A well-written profile of Tranquillo Cremona (1837–78), a distinguished artist, can be read in the *Enciclopedia Italiana di Scienze, Lettere e Arti*, 36 vols. (Rome, 1929–37), 11:832. See also Barbiera, and the graceful piece written by the artist Plinio Nomellini entitled '*L'Edera*' in *La Nazione*, 1935, no. 150. Furthermore, read what L. Beltrami wrote on the subject, and on Catalani, in *Il Marzocco*, 1935, no. 18. [Cremona's picture has been reproduced in most books on the composer, and can be readily found on the internet. Catalani is the 'ivy' of the painting's title; he is shown clinging to a blonde girl. The painting was made in 1878, when Catalani was still in relatively good health. ED.]

2 The appointment commenced by Royal Decree on 11 April 1888.

3 [Letter to Giuseppe Depanis, 3 August 1890. Letters 81. ED.] See also Catalani's students' recollections in *Gazzetta Musicale*, 1890.

4 Depanis.

included Mario Tarenghi, Carlo Gatti and Gaetano Luporini, all of whom excelled in their field.[1]

VI

DESPITE LIVING away from Lucca, Catalani missed his home-town hugely. He often spoke with affection of Lucca and was very keen to have his works performed there. It was when re-hearsals were taking place for *Loreley* at Rome's Teatro Argentino that he asked a journalist, probably Carlo Paladini, to say hello to Lucca, *where a big part of himself still resided.*[2]

When making short visits to relatives and old school friends he always made a point of seeing composers like Carlo Angeloni, Augusto Michelangeli, Carlo Giorgi, Ferruccio Ferrari and oth-ers who between the years 1880 and 1893 kept the musical torch of Lucca burning brightly.

Catalani had also promised that he would write a symphonic work for the Boccherini Orchestral Society, which between the

---

1 For Mario Tarenghi, a praiseworthy teacher and very decent composer, see Andrea Della Corte and Guido M. Gatti, *Dizionario di Musica* (Turin, 1925), and Alberto De Angelis, *L'Italia Musicale d'Oggi* (Rome, 1918).

Carlo Gatti is known for his valuable critical works and music. He is the editor of the very important series, *I Grandi Musicisti Italiani e Stranieri*, published in Milan. His biography of Giuseppe Verdi, published in 1931, is well worth a read. He has been teaching harmony and counterpoint at the Milan Conservatory since 1898. In a letter written to the Chief Justice of Lucca in 1932 Gatti expressed his opinion of Catalani thus: 'An artist who has left an indelible impression on the history of music, he personifies spiritual refinement, kindness and grace.'

For Gaetano Luporini see Rinaldo Cortopassi, 'Glorie musicali lucchesi: Gaetano Luporini' in *Artiglio*, 1935. [Luporini (1865–1948) enjoyed some success as an opera composer, his first opera, *Marcella*, being performed in 1891. His second, *I Dispetti Amorosi* (1894), had a libretto by Luigi Illica, who had written *La Wally* for Catalani. By the end of his life Catalani had come to see Luporini as something of a rival. Letters 133. ED.]

2 *Il Figurinaio*, 1893.

years 1890 and 1892 was enjoying burgeoning success for the wonderful concerts it organised.

In 1888 it seemed that Catalani's dream of seeing one of his works staged in his native town was about to come true. A townsman had put the idea of staging *Edmea* forward to the council, amongst other projects. The authorities even sought Catalani's advice on who he wanted to cast in the opera.[1] But it was not to be, and in the end the project was abandoned in favour of *Mefistofele* and *Lucrezia Borgia*, with Medea Borelli taking the lead role.[2] Catalani was distraught, particularly in view of the fact that *Edmea* was scheduled for performances in Genoa and Madrid, which attested to the opera's quality and importance.

Edmea was eventually to be performed in Lucca, but a journalist quite rightly wrote in a local paper in 1892 that the city, the birthplace of Catalani, 'had taken little care of this son of hers' and that, shamefully, not a single work of his 'had yet been performed at the Teatro Giglio.'[3]

It should be added that this type of indifference was frequently encountered by the vast majority of Lucca's talented and prodigious sons who excelled in the arts. They saw the value of their work undermined by intrigue, plots, professional envy, and politics.

It was not until 1892 that Catalani, whose talent and artistry had already caused such a stir, had the satisfaction of seeing one of his works performed in Lucca.

The town council had chosen *La Wally* for performance in September 1892, with the extraordinary Luisa Gilboni taking

---

1 The impresario was almost certainly Bartolomeo Mechetti. *Il Progresso*, 1888.

2 Medea Borelli was from Lucca. She was a distinguished and greatly admired soprano who turned to teaching bel canto with much success.

3 *Il Figurinaio*, 1892.

the lead role under the baton of Arturo Toscanini.[1] The decision attracted controversy, as reported in the local press. It was maintained in no uncertain terms that a standard repertory opera was needed for economic reasons. Before the opera had been definitively chosen, one newspaper came out with the polemical assertion that: 'The town council will not be influenced by the opinion of impresarios, and believes that in order to promote a fellow citizen of Lucca, albeit an illustrious composer worthy of exposure, it cannot dismiss other fine composers, all of whom have a right to have their works performed at the Teatro Giglio.'[2]

The statement received considerable support, and the matter was not to rest there. The Director of the newspaper, despite being a man of notable intelligence, angrily voiced his concerns with the town council advisory panel, of which he happened to be a member, belittling Catalani's music and thus fuelling the controversy.[3] All this should have been avoided, particularly as while this was happening all those involved were having petty tantrums directed at those siding politically with the opposing faction. Throughout the dispute there were intellectuals hailing from Lucca who defended Catalani. Names that spring to mind include the lawyer Enrico Del Carlo (*Leo*), and the distinguished poet Ferruccio Pieri (*P*). Yet in the heat of discussion the whole affair went off the rails. The usual logomachies, with unfortunate

---

1 Catalani had quite correctly predicted the splendid arrival of Toscanini on the international stage. Eraclio Gerbella, who taught at the Parma Conservatory, was the chorus master, and he was an excellent choice. [It is worth noting that by this juncture Toscanini and Catalani were close friends. See John W. Klein's fascinating article, 'Toscanini and Catalani – A Unique Friendship,' *Music and Letters* 48 (1967), 213-28. ED.]

2 *L'Esare*, 1892.

3 The Director was the Marquis Lorenzo Bottini, a combative man and shrewd polemicist. An interestingly scandalous and informative profile of him was written by the erudite Eugenio Lazzareschi. See *Atti della Reale Accademia Lucchese* New Series 1 (Lucca, 1931), xvii.

and peevish remarks, infect the journalism of a small city when the writers abandon decorum.[1]

Strangely, the newspaper which set the dispute off had in the past always recognised and praised Catalani's successes, but in its 'polemic article' now distanced itself from a critical consensus which amounted to such a positive endorsement of the opera that even those opposed to Catalani were forced to recognise it.[2] It had said earlier that the score represented 'an innovative creation of a new school of composition; most refined, delicate, heartfelt and gentle, and very descriptive, too!'[3] Journalists can be so contradictory!

Catalani was distressed by the whole affair, and also by the fact that the public was not flocking to the opera house in their hordes.[4] He bemoaned the fact to his closest friends.

Nevertheless, the opera was a success and favourably judged. Some boldly claimed that it was a masterpiece, and Catalani was hailed as the 'Benvenuto Cellini of music.'[5] However some of

---

1 See in particular *L'Esare*, 1892 and 1893. The debate was also contested in '*Il Paladino*' from *Il Figurinaio*, 1892. Enrico Del Carlo, a writer and politician, and Ferruccio Pieri, a refined and admired poet, both deserve to be remembered for their widely-read and valuable works. [Del Carlo (1843–1920) was Mayor of Lucca from 1888 to 1896, and represented the city in the Italian Parliament from 1876. Pieri (1864–1933) was a postal worker who wrote poetry in his spare time; he published his first volume of verse in 1893. ED.]

2 *L'Esare*, 1892.

3 *L'Esare*, 1892. See *Il Figurinaio*, 1892 for further opinions on the work. The opera was performed in Genoa with the famous Romanian soprano Hariclea Darclée. A review of the performance, written for *Il Caffaro*, can be read in *Il Progresso*, 1892.

4 Pardini added a long note here, detailing the nightly takings for the performances of *La Wally*. This is Appendix 3, '*La Wally* in Lucca, 1892: The Accounts,' pp. 87–88.

5 *Il Figurinaio*, 1892.

the townspeople were unsupportive, because of the unfortunate controversy leading up to the performances.

Catalani won the plaudits, most notably on the first night, of audiences who showered him with applause, and showed their appreciation of his great talent. Deeply moved, his eyes moistened and he spoke with emotion: 'I shall die content! I've achieved the ideals of my life!'[1] He had a deep attachment to Lucca, a city that had not always been entirely benevolent to him!

On the evening chosen to honour Catalani, the audience was not as numerous as desired; but the local cognoscenti, those most appreciative of the beauty and wisdom of art, were there.

Those who were by the Maestro's side, and could see how he was feeling, felt for him. The Mayor of Lucca, the lawyer Enrico Del Carlo who had demonstrated unfailing support for the opera,[2] presented Catalani with a crown and the following homily:

> *Lucca, 17 September 1892*
> *Illustrious Maestro,*
> *With a joyful heart I present you with this crown as a token of the esteem and affection in which you are held by the townspeople of Lucca. We have all been privileged to attend the performances of* La Wally, *a most inspired and skilful work.*
> *We sincerely hope that you, a good and sensitive man, will accept this modest yet precious gift offered you by your hometown, a hometown that acclaims you unanimously and with deeply felt emotion as one of the greatest composers to bring honour to Italy.*[3]

---

1 For the opera's opening night refer to the following local papers: *L'Esare, Il Progresso, Il Fulmine Secondo,* and *Il Figurinaio,* 1892.

2 Catalani was, oddly, confused about this. See Introduction, p. 7, note. ED.

3 *Il Progresso,* 1892.

Standing next to the Mayor was Carlo Giorgi, who on this occasion granted Catalani honorary membership of the Boccherini Orchestral Society, an honour of which the composer was most proud.[1]

Catalani grasped the rather modest crown presented by the Mayor between his frail hands, as if clinging to it, and as his huge eyes, betraying all his physical pain and internal anguish, turned toward the stalls and boxes, not overly crowded, he seemed numbed by the applause. He mustered the strength to utter the words 'thank you' with pale and quivering lips. It was an unforgettable scene!

The audience was not as enthusiastic about the opera as it should have been. The official ceremony, preceding the performance, had temporarily cooled the atmosphere, yet the audience was soon to warm up with the excerpts from other works by Catalani, which were also performed on this memorable evening.[2]

It is my duty to show respect for those who are no longer with us. I will not detail the full story of this event, nor will I unveil the full implications of the controversy. The editorial offices of the various newspapers involved in this unfortunate business knew full well the causes and machinations behind it, but did not disclose these fully to the public. Catalani could hardly have received worse treatment from his hometown, despite the

---

1 Carlo Giorgi was a great admirer of Catalani's work. He had conducted performances of the Mass many times, and was at this time President of the Boccherini Orchestral Society. The letter conferring Catalani's honorary membership stated that *La Wally* was 'a work that will defy the critics and the passing of time. It is a glorious work of Italian culture.' (See *L'Esare*, 1892 no. 75.) Catalani received, in addition to his crown, some gifts from friends and admirers.

2 The Dance of the Ondines from *Loreley* and the Prelude to Act IV of *Dejanice* were played, both pieces being encored much to the delight of the audience. The romanza from *Edmea* was also performed, in honour of the baritone Mario Ancona (*L'Esare*, 1892).

honour he had brought to it with his work, and in particular with *La Wally*.

Del Carlo wrote with acumen when he stated that the opera was 'the work of a skilled maestro,' adding that '*La Wally* is a strong, passionate, truthful work, the liveliness of its plot intensified by an extraordinary unity.'[1]

Ferruccio Pieri, a contemporary of Catalani's and the finest poet from Lucca, the precision of whose work particularly delights, and who in time will be rewarded with the widespread recognition he deserves, eulogised the composer with the following words:

> *A wave of harmonies calmly descends*
> *Through the body, the senses, agitating*
> *With the potency of dulcet notes:*
> *A wave in which your name shines clearly.*[2]

VII

THE COMPOSER'S health was waning visibly, day by day. With heavy heart I quote the following from the journal *La Tribuna*: 'When Catalani travelled to Rome last year to attend performances of his *Loreley* he hardly seemed to be among the living. He was a slim, pale figure, with an incurable pallor revealing his diminished vitality. His sunken eyes gazed pitifully around, stunned to find themselves resting on a crowd of people alive and well. His whole being, exhausted even by the smallest physical effort, his voice and gait showing signs of spirit only during moments of artistic expression, revealed how he was barely clutching at life. It was as though a puff of wind could have blown him into the land of shadows.'[3]

---

1 *Il Progresso*, 1892.

2 Ibid.

3 *La Tribuna*, 1893. *Il Fulmine Secondo*, 1893.

Yet despite his physical debility Catalani clung to feelings of hope and life: he fervently yearned to continue his work in the theatre.[1] Tender melodies resonated in his heart; the beauty inherent in art flourished in his soul. He was restless, urged on by his innate creativity, and wrote that his new opera 'will be in three acts and will be entitled *Nella Selva* [*In the woods*]. The culminating scene is taken from Tolstoy.'[2]

This was a big project, incorporating the work of a giant literary figure, the immortal Russian author of lengthy, powerful novels. Catalani wanted to keep going, and in that body of his, falling into decline, his mind, imagination and creativity sought hard work as a refuge.

While travelling through the Saint Gotthard mountain, Catalani coughed up blood, a sign that the end was coming.[3] And it came, on 7 August 1893. The black veil draped over the

---

1 Catalani had a passionate desire to work. He thought about work the whole time, to the extent that he became so distracted he wasn't even aware of where he was. He had a great memory for all his musical ideas. See p. 29, note 1.

2 Letter to Giuseppe Depanis, 20 June 1893. Letters 136. For more on this planned opera see below, p. 101 and note. ED.

3 The Gotthard Rail Tunnel opened in 1882. Depanis had reported that Catalani coughed up blood and was forced to abandon his journey on 2 August (30). According to Catalani's later biographer, Severino Pagani, Catalani was travelling to Faido in Switzerland: *Alfredo Catalani: Ombre e luci nella sua Vita e nella sua Arte* (Milan, 1957), 168. Gatti says that Catalani left Milan on 1 August (235), though it is unclear whether he had independent authority for this, or was simply making an educated guess on the basis of Depanis's date. Cortopassi claims that Catalani left Milan on 28 July and only got as far as the frontier station of Chiasso before he was forced to return (227–28). The immediate background to this final trip is described in full by Nappi: see below, pp. 99–102. Summer trips to the mountains and lakes, in a hopeless quest for better health, were a regular part of Catalani's life. He had been to Faido before, in August 1890, when he wrote to Giuseppe Depanis 'I'm here in the mountains, trying to reinvigorate myself a little and to become a little fatter, if it's possible.' Letters 81. ED.

corpse shrouded one of Italy's greatest glories. His last days were chronicled by Illica in a heart-rending letter to Alfredo Caselli, from which I quote:[1] 'I, too, cannot get used to the fact of Catalani's death. He had finally started to work again, to work hectically, but with the energy of one who forbodes that death awaits him around the corner!

'His final days were horrific! When alert and aware of his physical condition he was in such agony. This suffering was followed by bouts of profound lethargy that led him to a state of total oblivion.

'In his final words he sorely lamented the great work he had been ruminating over, but in his last moments, as death loomed large, he felt some relief:

'"It is she! ... It is death ... ah, at long last, the end is in sight! Such a pity! I have the music here in my heart ... yes, here! Farewell, La Scala! ... Farewell libretto by Illica ... I feel so cold ... Yet I'm beginning to feel well!"'

'And Catalani passed away in lucid awareness of what was happening, with a sense of resignation and contentment. His pain in those last hours must have been excruciating, his feeble body losing its final battle for life.

'I maintain he died a happy man, and I really do believe it. The pain he was having to endure had been so severe that the day before his death he tried to end it all by throwing himself off his bed, and Toscanini had great difficulty exhorting him to lay down again.

---

1 Pardini cites no source for this letter. It had been published by Carlo Paladini as a 'P.S.' to his article 'Un Maestro di musica e due Poeti da teatro: Alcune lettere inedite di Alfredo Catalani,' *Musica e Musicisti* 58 (1903), 1041–47. Paladini records that he was checking through his article in a café in Lucca; Caselli came in, saw what he was doing, and promptly hurried off to fetch this important letter from Illica. Paladini wrote of the letter: 'Who can read these words, flying sparks of pain and brotherly tenderness, without feeling tears well up in their eyes?' For Paladini, see pp. 12 and 133–36.

'He was acutely aware of his suffering, his mind still very lucid, and he was reasoning with all his mental faculties, so his throwing himself off his bed was a genuine attempt at suicide. Catalani was hoping for a loss of consciousness to cut short his torture.[1]

'Ferrario and I washed his corpse and dressed him. We lay him down on his freshly made deathbed and scattered flowers around his body. No funeral director touched the body of the artist; Ferrario and I felt a deep satisfaction in performing this duty ourselves.'[2]

Even in death, and I sincerely hope my repeating this does not seem ironic, Catalani was only 'half lucky.'

The funeral itself was a most modest affair, yet it did little to detract from Catalani's value as a musician and man who had always shunned ostentation in any shape or form. When Enrico Del Carlo, the Mayor, gave, on behalf of the townspeople of Lucca, the final salute in front of the corpse, no one from Milan or the Conservatory spoke. Giulio Ricordi, appalled by this unsympathetic display, gave the 'final and sincere' concise and stirring speech.[3] This painful episode in the life of the composer

---

1 Intriguingly, Pardini omits a paragraph here: 'His [Catalani's] death was also the death of a strong man. He wished to be cremated. But understanding that his family would be saddened by such a decision, he yet again abandoned one of his most cherished desires.' ED.

2 Catalani's uncle Felice, his cousins on his mother's side, Giovanni and Enrichetta Picconi, with whom he was living, the poet Luigi Illica, Arturo Toscanini and Professor Ferrario were with Catalani during his final days of agony. Professor Ferrario, the distinguished clinician, was Catalani's physician and a great admirer.

3 This is what Ricordi said, more or less, and it produced an immense effect: 'Silence is without question the greatest proof of the pain and suffering surrounding us, oh poor Catalani. But as no one has given you a final salute on behalf of the city where you lived, and that respected and applauded your work, let it be me that bids you this final and sincere farewell, from the bottom of my heart.' *Gazzetta Musicale*, 1893.

of so many enduring and wondrous works shall remain with me forever.[1]

One authoritative voice was not silent on this occasion, the voice of the greatest Italian composer, a genius, and warm-spirited man: Giuseppe Verdi. In a letter written to Edoardo Mascheroni he said: 'Poor Catalani! He was a good man and excellent musician! How distressing it all is! Do congratulate Giulio for those few and beautiful words he spoke about that poor man!

'Shame and guilt upon the others!'[2]

The citizens of Lucca expressed their wish to have the corpse taken to Lucca, so Catalani could be buried next to other members of his family.[3] The local authorities duly agreed to this posthumous tribute to their celebrated son, and made arrangements for the coffin to be transported to Lucca. Yet they were slow to move, as a letter by Felice, Catalani's uncle, addressed to Del Carlo, testifies: 'I can only deduce from your prolonged silence that nothing has been settled yet with the Milanese authorities.

'I am most aggrieved by this delay, which gravely compromises his wretched remains,[4] and I ask you to notify me of what I hope will be a decision in the imminent future. If no progress is made then, I shall have no alternative but to bury his corpse in the Milan cemetery permanently.'[5]

---

1 See Depanis, Barbiera, *L'Esare*, 1893, *Il Progresso*, 1893.

2 Barbiera.

3 Catalani had himself made it known that he wanted to be buried next to his family. [But see p. 77, note 1. ED.]

4 The body had been placed in a poor wooden coffin and temporarily left at the cemetery in Milan. [See Nappi's account below, pp. 103 and 122. ED.]

5 At this time the close artistic circle in which Catalani moved in Milan commemorated his life with a memorial concert. Many distinguished soloists performed in the concert, which was attended by the artistic elite. *L'Esare*, 1894.

The bureaucratic hurdles finally overcome, on 16 March 1894 Catalani's coffin was at long last interred, in accordance with the wishes of the citizens of Lucca, in his hometown.[1]

I feel it is right and proper to repeat what was written in a local paper when the coffin arrived in Lucca, on a wet and gloomy day: 'The angels keeping watch over the deceased composer were weeping.'[2] The unfortunate artist, who had suffered so much, who was a good man and a Christian, really did deserve to be wept over, especially by those who could express their grief with celestial melodies.[3]

I have now accomplished what I initially set out to do.

It is not my intention to offer a character analysis of the Maestro, who has been so succinctly and masterfully described by Giuseppe Depanis in his book, and latterly by other writers who knew him for many years and were intimately acquainted with his thoughts, his ambitions, his life. Nor will I investigate the reasons behind the unspoken enmity that was said to exist between him and Puccini.[4]

---

1 For details about the funeral procession see in particular *L'Esare, Il Progresso* and *Il Fulmine Secondo*, 1894.

2 *Il Fulmine Secondo*, 1894.

3 The city band performed some funeral marches composed by Carlo Giorgi, 'one of which was written especially for the occasion, making use of a motif taken from the start of Act IV of *La Wally*.' *L'Esare*, 1894.

The Catalani Society, which was inaugurated on 1 February 1894 in the composer's honour, also participated in the event.

4 Puccini took part in Catalani's funeral procession in Lucca. When the idea of erecting a monument in Catalani's honour was mooted he wrote: 'I applaud the noble idea of erecting a monument to Alfredo Catalani in his city, to Alfredo Catalani, the distinguished and original musician who has left behind much sorrow, making his all-too-brief life on earth an eternal memory etched in the souls of all those who understood and loved the man who was so gentle and poetic.' [This quotation is slightly paraphrased from Puccini's letter to Enrico Lippi of 16 May 1900, reproduced in *Onoranze*, 14. See Introduction, p. 2. ED.]

Nor shall I talk about 'the lady who had a bust cast in bronze of her beloved which she donated to the Milan Conservatory. This gentle soul was never to forget her poor Alfredo.'[1] And how he deserved this sweet and enduring remembrance because of his kindness, modesty, culture and all his wonderful talents. Even with his poor health, Catalani knew how to awaken the fondness, luminous and gentle, so much liked by ladies, which transforms itself into love.

Silence reigned over Catalani's works for some considerable time, but the great artist Arturo Toscanini, who much admired the composer and still does, revived the works that had made men shed tears and hearts flutter with their 'sweet notes, that the heart forgot, then recognised, and forever remembered.'[2]

---

1 Barbiera. [For this lady, see below, pp. 89–92. For a photograph of the bust see p. 124. ED.]

2 The beautiful epigraph written by Giovanni Pascoli in 1900 is mounted on the house in Via Santa Giustina where Catalani lived during his youth: 'To Alfredo Catalani – the consoler of souls – born in Lucca 19 June 1854 – died in Milan 7 August 1893 – the Guido Monaco Music Society – celebrates his memory – on the XXV anniversary of its foundation – 24 May MCM.

'In his all-too-brief life – he gazed high above – and wrote with heaven-sent inspiration *Dejanice, Edmea, Loreley* and *La Wally* – shedding on men the sweet notes – that the heart forgot, then recognised, and forever remembered.

'The harp hangs from the weeping willow, yet its strings ring true, plucked by fingers our eyes no longer see.'

Great souls meet and understand each other.

Displayed on the plaque is a portrait of Catalani. It is an accomplished work of art by the distinguished sculptor Francesco Petroni.

[Giovanni Pascoli (1855–1912) was coming to be recognised as one of Italy's foremost poets at this time; he is renowned for both his Italian and Latin poetry. He was asked to write the epigraph by Alfredo Caselli, a friend of both Pascoli and Catalani (Alfredo Catalani 160). Francesco Petroni (1877–1960) was a young sculptor from Lucca who later gained a national reputation; the bronze medallion of Catalani reproduced on the cover of this book is his work. ED.]

Carlo D'Ormeville wrote: 'When future generations cast their eyes over the scores of this Maestro from Lucca they will realize that he was the greatest musician of the nineteenth century.'[1] Well, perhaps! Nevertheless, the accomplished composer of *Loreley* and *La Wally* shall forever occupy a prime position. With great skill he instilled a feeling and humanity in these works that moved men deeply.

A true masterpiece never dies. It may be neglected temporarily, sometimes because of the bizarre twists and turns of fashion, or because of the envy and personal ambitions of the mediocre. But its light will break through the clouds when one least expects it.

Cultural development is crucially important, and I agree wholeheartedly with the distinguished critic Andrea Della Corte, who in an authoritative statement on Mozart said: 'Yes, culture also must be founded upon total conviction, with strong examples and sound methods, as in the music of Mozart or Rossini, or Wagner or Bellini. And Italy could easily revive dozens of beautiful operas and their composers. But cultural fashion plays an important role, and the traditions and taste that created those works have been lost.'[2]

Catalani's music is sure to triumph, and imminently, as testified by the promising inroads it is making today. And it is he and the many other great composers hailing from Lucca that make their city duly proud of its unique heritage, which surely cannot be gainsaid.

---

1 Pardini gives no source for this amazing statement, but it is taken from the 1900 *Onoranze*, in a report of a speech by Enrico Lippi in celebration of Catalani. Lippi prefaced it with the introduction: 'In a biography of Catalani, the poet and scholar Carlo D'Ormeville says ...' (77). I have been unable to discover where, or if, this biography – potentially a valuable primary source – was published. Pardini makes no mention of it, and nor do later biographers. ED.

2 'Si parla di Mozart,' *La Nazione*, 1934, no. 123.

The fame of Catalani and Puccini, both outstanding musicians, shall conquer the centuries. They created music bathed in light and glory that touches men's hearts. And let us not forget a third Tuscan, the brilliant and powerful composer Pietro Mascagni, prolific in his output, who will also be famed and honoured for his work.

These eminent artists, the pride and glory of Tuscany and Italy, while responsive to the technical progress of modern music, expressed their genius with their beloved and timeless melodies. They composed melodies that encapsulate beauty, in all its glory and pain. Music that strove with unabated fervour to overcome life's trials and tribulations. It brings consolation, and in its harmony is a reflection of our beloved homeland, where

> *There's joy in the sea, the skies, and mountains*
> *Nature is touched by paradise!*[1]

---

1 The quotation is from the poem 'La patria dell' Italiano' ('The Homeland of the Italians') by Antonio Gazzoletti (1813–66). ED.

Appendix 1: Catalani's Family Background

THE FOLLOWING information was gleaned from parish records:

The family lived in Via San Salvatore, now Via Asili. The family unit in 1853 and 1854 consisted of:

Catalani, Eugenio, son of Domenico, music teacher, 28 years of age;

Giuseppa,[1] daughter of Vincenzo Picconi, his wife, 28 years of age;

Roberto, their son, 1 year of age.

Living with the family was Giuseppa's sister, 18 years of age, and a maid.

In 1855 the family had another member, the 1 year-old Alfredo.

It is quite possible that Giuseppa's sister was married in 1856, leading the family to move to Via San Giustina to live with Eugenio's parents. The parish records for 1856 contain the following:

Catalani, Domenico, music teacher, son of Felice and Stella Sani, 66 years of age;

Rosaria, his wife, daughter of Andrea Mariani and Lucia Romboni, 50 years of age;

Felice, unmarried son, 29 years of age;

Eugenio, son, 31 years of age;

Giuseppa, wife, 31 years of age;

Roberto, their son, 4 years of age;

Alfredo, their son, 2 years of age.

---

1 In his main text Pardini consistently refers to Catalani's mother as Giuseppina, as do later biographers. It appears, then, that this was the name she ordinarily used; but that she had been christened Giuseppa. ED.

Alfredo was born in a house owned by the Marquis A. Tucci in Via San Salvatore, which later became Via Asili, not in Via San Giustina, as some erroneously believe. This fact is clearly stated in the *Corriere Toscano* for 1900 and also in the newspaper *Esare*, edition no. 117, 1900.[1]

---

[1] Since Pardini wrote new information about the Catalani family has been unearthed. See, in particular, Nicola Laganà's account in Alfredo Catalani, 41ff. ED.

Appendix 2: Catalani's Teacher, Fortunato Magi

Fortunato Magi was born in Lucca on 6 October 1839 and died of serious brain disease in Venice on 27 May 1882. He studied music and counterpoint under his brother-in-law, Michele Puccini. In his all-too-brief life he composed some good works, and was an accomplished teacher and conductor. He made his mark in a variety of important posts because of his superior intelligence and professional perseverance. He became Director of the Istituto Musicale Pacini, but relinquished the post because of disagreements with the public officials of Lucca (*Il Fedele*, 1873). He subsequently took up posts in Sarzana, Ferrara and Spezia, and was finally appointed Artistic Director and Professor of Harmony and Counterpoint at the Liceo Benedetto Marcello in Venice, a position he held for five years, from 1877 to 1882. Prominent musicians who studied under him include Antonio de Lorenzi Fabris, Candido Radi, Giulio Tirindelli, Francesco De Guarnieri, Gino Buzzolla and Silvio Boscarini, the conductor.

The following is an excerpt from a speech by the President of the Liceo Benedetto Marcello, Count Contin di Castelseprio, delivered at the composer's funeral on 29 May 1882:

'Magi was endowed with a complex and spiritual temperament which facilitated his great aptitude for music. This temperament, combined with an apposite and meticulous study of the music of the old masters, and in particular of the masterpieces of sacred music, put to good use at a very early age, enabled him to win plaudits later in life from admirers both in Italy and abroad.

'He became known in the musical institutions of his home-town, Lucca, as well as those of Ferrara and Spezia, for his accomplished music, and many of his compositions testify to his thorough technique and masterly command of counterpoint. And when Venice's Liceo Marcello was founded it was he who was chosen to teach his subject, which he knew so well, and in this post he was held in high esteem.

'He was also most highly regarded for his kindly disposition and genial ways while performing his onerous duties at the helm of the newly founded institution, a position he maintained with great ability and uncustomary devotion ...'

Magi's music is remembered by Luigi Nerici, F. J. Fétis and countless others who wrote about him in both the local and national press.

The current Director of the Liceo Marcello has informed me that an undated manuscript is kept in the Institute of Magi's 'Preludio per grande orchestra.'[1]

Further information can be found in the following books and newspapers: Nerici; Schmidl; Luigi Landucci, *Carlo Angeloni: Cronistoria* (Lucca, 1905); *Il Serchio*, 1870, 1873; *La Provincia di Lucca*, 1872, 1877; *Il Progresso*, 1882; *La Gazzetta di Venezia*, 1882.

---

1 Remarkably, this 'Preludio' has been recorded: it can be found on the Multipromo disc, *Omaggio a Giacomo Puccini* (MPR012). In addition, two of Magi's motets and a 'Sinfonia con grande orchestra e banda' have been released on a Bongiovanni disc that also includes a large scale 'Miserere' by Carlo Angeloni (GB 5030-2). ED.

Appendix 3: *La Wally* in Lucca, 1892: The Accounts

A NATIVE OF Lucca, Mr. Casimiro Barsotti, made a collection of articles and documents related to the history and artistic heritage of the city. This is stored in files now kept in the Library and State Archive of Lucca. I extract a list of the takings for the evening performances of *La Wally* at Lucca in 1892, and the expenses incurred by the impresario, Scattini. This makes for highly entertaining and interesting reading.

Takings	4	September 1892	Lire	975.40
//	6	//	//	472.85
//	8	//	//	781.60
//	10	//	//	451.00
//	11	//	//	674.15
//	13	//	//	566.40
//	14[1]	//	//	1321.90
//	17	//	//	966.10
//	18	//	//	714.50
//	20	//	//	265.10
//	21	//	//	154.15
//	24	//	//	525.10
//	25	//	//	490.60
Grant from the City			//	6000.00
Total			//	**14358.85**

---

1 On this evening the audience included many people from outside Lucca.

Expenses	Company	Lire	6760.00
"	Chorus (Male)	"	1566.00
"	Chorus (Female)	"	1943.75
"	Set Hire	"	376.00
"	Equipment	"	188.00
"	Music	"	1305.36
"	Costumes	"	1116.80
"	Shoes	"	51.70
"	Tarlatan	"	65.75
"	Orchestra (local players)	"	2080.00
"	Orchestra (others)	"	4184.40
"	Duty staff	"	905.19
"	Stage setup	"	250.00
"	Chorus Master	"	520.00
"	Tax	"	350.00
"	Carlo Giorgi (Assistant Director)	"	100.00
"	2 Chorus Extras	"	72.80
"	Horn Player (for 32 days)	"	96.00
"	Miscellaneous	"	763.30
"	**Total**	"	22695.05

The expenses incurred by the impresario for putting together the company, its travel expenses, telegrams and hotel accommodation are not included in this list.

Appendix 4: Catalani's Loves
David Chandler

CATALANI SEEMS to have had at least three or four romantic relationships, all of them shrouded in considerable mystery. The first, allegedly, was with one Oretta, a niece of the Italian Pardini family with whom he stayed in Paris in the early 1870s. Rinaldo Cortopassi, the first writer to mention this, cited the authority of the conductor Carlo Carignani (1857–1919), who claimed to have known Oretta. Cortopassi's book, published in 1954, remains the only authority for this early romance. He was, depending on point of view, an excitingly speculative or completely irresponsible biographer, and it is all but impossible to say where fact shades off into novelistic elaboration in his account. He describes Catalani writing the earliest version of 'Ebben? Ne andrò lontana' for Oretta as a farewell gift (47), imagines the composer struggling to forget her when back in Italy, has Oretta meeting Catalani backstage when *Dejanice* was performed in Nice in 1886 (145), and cites a report that she died around 1890, with Catalani's name on her lips (219). Cortopassi clearly believed, or wanted to believe, that Oretta was the great love of Catalani's life.

There can be little doubt, however, that Catalani's most important romantic relationship was with Teresa Junck, née Garbagnati (died 1928), the wife of his friend, the minor composer Benedetto Junck (1852–1903). As it was not an open affair, very little indeed is known about it. The first published hint of the relationship seems to have come from Raffaello Barbiera, who in his 1926 account of Catalani translated here describes the composer's coffin 'as showered with flowers given by the lady who had a bust cast in bronze of her beloved which she donated to the Milan Conservatory. This gentle soul was never to forget her poor Alfredo.' For anyone prepared to make enquires this was enough to identify Teresa, for it was she who, in 1908, five

years after her husband's death, commissioned three busts of
Catalani from the sculptor Achille Alberti, one of which she
donated to the Milan Conservatory, and one to La Scala (her
own copy was left to the City of Lucca).[1] Pardini, who cites
Barbiera on the 'bronze bust,' almost certainly knew something
of the relationship, but contented himself with a general statement about Catalani's ability to inspire womanly love. In his 1953
biography, Carlo Gatti hinted much more strongly at a romantic
and illicit relationship, though without explicitly saying that one
took place. He described Catalani's visits to the artistic gather-
ings at the Juncks' home, and imagined him playing parts of
Elda there:

> In her songs, Elda appears as an image of
> love conjured up in the dreams of this young
> composer.
>   With ardent passion, Teresa makes those
> songs her own and her young musician loses
> himself in her, his art personifying her. (85)

The reference to *Elda* is significant, because it clearly suggests
that in Gatti's understanding the affair between Catalani and
Teresa began early, probably around 1880.

Later writers on Catalani have assumed that the affair took
place and that cryptic references to a certain 'Signora T' in his
letters refer to Teresa. Just one known letter reveals something
of his feelings for her. This was written to the singer Virginia
Ferni, who was in on the secret, when Catalani was ill with flu
in January 1890:

> Ah! I can't rest for not having been able to
> see her [Teresa], although I understand the
> reasons why she didn't come up [to visit me]!

---

1 Aldo Berti gives a full account of these busts in Alfredo Catalani 161–3.
A photograph of the Lucca bust is reproduced below, p. 124.

Teresa Junck

Tell her that I'm always alone ... that I can
never tire of telling her so many things that
she will like, and of showing her something
that she certainly doesn't expect, but which
will certainly be the most eloquent proof that,
if I apparently behaved badly and indelicately
toward her (in a moment when the emptiness
and discomfort which the feeling of loneliness
causes frightened me), at the bottom of my
heart I have never for an instant stopped feeling for her that devotion and affection that she
alone has known how to inspire in my life,
an affection which has now been increased by
regret at having caused her to suffer so much.
Tell her that I'm awaiting a word of peace and
forgiveness from her ... and that if she doesn't
want to do this for me, she should do it for my
art, which I will never be able to stop personi-
fying in her.[1]

John Klein took this statement at face value when he boldly
declared that Teresa was 'the only woman' Catalani 'ever pas-
sionately loved.'[2] It may be so, but Catalani was obviously
anxious to say something meaningful, his own emotions were
clearly confused, and some caution is required.

Like most similar affairs, Catalani's with Teresa was probably unsatisfactory, and as the years passed he began to yearn
for something more substantial. Sometime early in 1886 he
referred to a recent romance, or perhaps infatuation, in a letter to Antonio Ghislanzoni that Pardini quotes: 'I even fell in

---

1 Letters 76.

2 John W. Klein, 'Toscanini and Catalani – A Unique Friendship,' *Music
and Letters* 48 (1967), 224.

love with a woman ... but I'll tell you the strange adventure in person.'[1] This is odd: it apparently refers to something that had taken place when *Dejanice* was being performed in Nice, and it was at precisely this juncture, it will be recalled, that Cortopassi claimed Catalani was reunited with Oretta. Possibly the reference is to Oretta, and Cortopassi (who quotes the letter) seems to have read it that way; but this is, to say the least, a strange way to refer to an old flame. There is also a slight – very slight – possibility that the letter refers to Catalani's cousin, Luisa Picconi, to whom he became engaged in 1889. On the whole, though, the balance of probability must be in favour of the 1886 letter referring to a so far unidentified woman.

Catalani announced his engagement to Luisa in a letter to Giuseppe Depanis of 30 October 1889:

> I'm telling it to you first, no one knows it yet. For two days I've been engaged to a little cousin of mine, a daughter of Picconi's. Don't think, my friend, that this is a step that I'm taking lightly, recklessly. No; for some time now I've been fed up with my life as a '*garçon*' [bachelor], all the more so since I don't have a father, mother, or siblings. I grew to like this girl, who is refined and intelligent, and who likes me very much, gradually. (So true is it that she likes me, that in less than a year, she has refused two excellent offers out of love for me.) I have allowed myself to be won over by the attractive prospect of a life that is quiet, and tranquil, and full of work. She well knows that my position, at the moment, is anything

---

1 Letters 24.

but splendid. But it doesn't matter; she has
told her parents: 'either he or no one,' and
her parents have consented. I'll tell you then
in person and at greater length so many par-
ticulars concerning this 'love story,' which can
really be called that.[1]

One must suspect that the 'love' was on Luisa's side and the
'story' on Catalani's, for the letter sounds much more like the
statement of a man pleased to have found someone willing to
marry him than deeply in love. The relationship is most likely
to have started in early autumn 1888, when Catalani was stay-
ing with the Picconi family,[2] and seems to have been mainly
conducted at a distance. The engagement only lasted a few
weeks; in late November 1889 Catalani became seriously ill
with bronchitis and, alarmed by the condition of his health,
Luisa's family decided to break off the match.[3] Luisa seems
to have loved Catalani as much as he claimed, and was not
prepared to give him up; her family consequently began to cast
aspersions on his moral character, leading him into an agony of
hurt, confused and resentful feelings.[4] At this juncture, having
apparently abandoned hope of Luisa, Catalani sent his urgent
reassurances to Teresa.

Life had come to strangely mirror art. *Loreley*, premiered
on 16 February 1890, had finally gone into production, with
its story of Walter torn between his engagement to the emi-
nently virtuous and suitable Anna and the wildwood charms of
Loreley. Walter's inconsistency causes him to lose both women,
and Catalani no doubt feared that his would have the same

---

1 Letters 69.

2 Letters 53.

3 Gatti 176.

4 See Catalani's letter to an unknown female correspondent of 27 January
1890. Letters 76–77.

result. It is not clear how Teresa responded to the appeal of January 1890, but the general tone of Catalani's later letters would suggest that she probably forgave her unhappy lover.

Alfredo Catalani, c. 1893
(This has been described as the 'final portrait' of Catalani.
See above, p. ix.)

In Memory of Alfredo Catalani

Giovanni Battista Nappi

[Originally published as a four-part article,
'In Memoriam Alfredo Catalani,' in the newspaper *La
Perseveranza* between 6 and 9 August 1918.]

TODAY MARKS the 25th Anniversary of Alfredo Catalani's death.[1]
Catalani retreated to the dust all too soon, yet in these last
twenty five years his name has not been erased, unlike the names
which can be scarcely made out on ancient tombs.[2]

In fact, with the passing of time his name has become increasingly prominent; the lettering, if anything, more legible. For the
music lovers of today Catalani has become a symbol of what is
immaculate in art.

The works he has left us are by no means voluminous; but
they are undoubtedly much more valuable than those of some
living composers, whose exuberant productivity is no indication
of real artistic talent.

So does Catalani's work require a hymn of praise rather than
the unwarranted disparagement hurled at it during the distinguished composer's lifetime? No, I don't think so.

---

1 Nappi follows this opening statement with a few poetical quotations
and reflections that have been omitted here.

2 An allusion to Petrarch's *Triumph of Death*, which Nappi has quoted.

It really is unnecessary for *La Perseveranza*, at least, to sing Catalani's praises. This newspaper is not guilty of having mis-understood or underestimated the value and completeness of his work.

Indeed it was Filippo Filippi who, in these very columns, hailed the young composer from Lucca with cordial eloquence as one of the great hopes of Italian music.[1] Later critics, with no claims of equalling the authority of their illustrious predecessor, are of the same opinion in their appraisals. We all believe that Catalani would have been able to create a wholly Italian music drama that would better respond to the exigencies of the music of today, and that would have dragged this musical genre away from the hybridity from which it has struggled to free itself for far too long.

It is such a pity that his untimely death halted his innovative music in its tracks, music that had started out so auspiciously.

Let us never forget this mournful anniversary. We can relive the memories by sketching Catalani's personal life and dwell-ing on certain episodes of his brief career only known to a few people. To this end, I shall be citing some of my personal recollections, presenting information kindly supplied to me by Catalani's friends and students, and gleaning knowledge from Giuseppe Depanis's excellent book, *I concerti popolari e il Teatro Regio di Torino*, which the publishers have kindly al-lowed me to quote.[2]

---

1 Filippo Filippi (1830–87), a very influential critic, had been appointed music and art critic of *La Perseveranza* in 1859 (Nappi succeeded him in the position). In a review of *La Falce*, published 19 July 1875, he praised Catalani enthusiastically. The composer long remembered this favourable notice, writing to Giuseppe Depanis on 18 November 1889: 'Filippi praised it [*La Falce*] to the seventh heaven.' Letters 70.

2 This had been published in 1915. The account of Catalani which it contains is mostly adapted from Depanis's 1893 biography.

The announcement of Catalani's final hours

AT DUSK on Sunday 6 August 1893 I received the following brief and distressing telegram from the office of the Spa in Regoledo, where I was sojourning for treatment:

> *'Maestro Catalani will not live another day,*
> *telegraph your obituary quickly.'*

It was signed by an editorial colleague unaware of the fact that his communication, sent in the late afternoon, had arrived just ten minutes before the Spa office was due to close.

Yet even given more time, how could anyone possibly sum up in fifty words or so all the artistic achievements of the dying composer?

Ill prepared and shocked by the news of his imminent demise, I was incapable – though I mustered all my strength the following day – of gathering my thoughts in order to express the calamity faced by Italian art with the passing away of Alfredo Catalani.

Remembering also that he had lived through many severe and recurring pulmonary attacks (and it was very unlikely he had fallen victim of yet another fatal illness), I was hoping this latest episode might yet again prove a false alarm.

A lethal mistake in Milan[1]

I FOUND IT hard to believe that Catalani was about to die, because I had been with him just twenty days earlier in Varese and had no inkling that he was so close to the end.

For some time past we had been used, unfortunately, to seeing him dragging himself around the streets and artists' dens

---

1 This section was actually published with the title 'A lethal mistake in Varese,' which seems to have been a mistake.

of Milan, his frail, skeletal body bent with the burden of life. We gazed with dismay at his lean face, haggard and cadaverous despite the prominence of his cheek bones, his large eyes glistening with the fever that plagued him in his final few months. His hair and drooping moustache, at one time the colour of ebony, were now as white as an eighty-year-old's, and he was just thirty-nine.

It was so distressing for us to hear him cough. It was a dry, barking, deep cough which exhausted him and caused him to bring a handkerchief anxiously to his lips; he would wipe it across his mouth and examine it furtively, eyeing it with trepidation, fearful of finding a trace of blood, a worrying symptom of hemoptysis, of which he suffered frequent bouts.

And yet we'd almost convinced ourselves that he was an exception: someone who famously always sought balance in his life, who despite being plagued by ill health never made the sort of mistake which could lead to the realm of death.

Indeed at Varese I found him in a seemingly positive frame of mind. He who was normally taciturn had become more talkative. He would smile more, and laughed with greater spontaneity, but not in a *strident way*, or *hiccupping sort of way* as Depanis claims, nor would I say that he showed any tendency to break off the conversation to *stare into the distance with dazed eyes*.

On that particular occasion he had a ready wit, one that was neither caustic nor malicious, the sort that those tormented by success and fate resort to (regrettably, he fell into this category). No, that day he had the lively and appealing sharpness of someone who looks at life through rose-tinted glasses.

He was happy. That was clear to see; he even said as much. It was as though he had forgotten all about his psychological and physical hardships, and the deafness that was adding to his distress.

He'd spoken of his anxiety on more than one occasion: 'My dear, I am going deaf; what will become of me? How will I be able to write music if my condition worsens?'

I would try to raise his spirits, attributing his loss of hearing to influenza, the symptoms of which would sooner or later disappear. But we all suspected the worst, fearing that this curse, too, was a result of the insidious enemy sapping his life away. That July, as I have already mentioned, his spirits were raised. He hinted at his latest project, which he was hoping to work on in October. He'd vowed to himself that he was going to set to work.

'Illica and Giovanni Pozza are writing a very beautiful libretto for me.[1] It is really all so exciting. I'll tell you soon what I propose calling the work, and what it is all about.'

These were Catalani's last words to me as we bid farewell at the station in Varese. He was heading for Lake Maggiore, where he was to spend some time in Premeno. But he was soon to change his mind. He returned to Milan just days later, quite possibly because he wanted to be in closer contact with his librettists.[2]

His demise was precipitated by an imprudence he committed while giving no thought, because of his reasonable state of health mentioned earlier, to the sword of Damocles hanging over his head.

---

1 Giovanni Pozza (1852–1914) was the music and theatre critic for the *Corriere della sera*. Catalani wrote to Illica on 8 May 1893: 'I have an outline for an opera; it is very beautiful and in three acts. I do, however, have to tell you immediately that I did not find it; Giovanni Pozza suggested it to me; he's completely in agreement with me in thinking that no one could adapt it for the stage and dress it in a poetic form better than you.' *Letters* 132. Two titles were considered for the opera: *Egor* and *Nella Selva* (*In the woods*).

2 Catalani wrote to Illica from Milan on 11 July 1893: 'This evening I'm going to Varese, and from there, for several days, to the mountains of Lake Maggiore.' *Letters* 138. In the end, he spent most of the following fortnight at Varese, writing from there to Illica on 18 July: 'I went to the mountains, but I had to come back because of the great cold' (ibid). He returned to Milan around 25 July.

Luigi Illica, who I will later leave to recount some interesting facts which have hitherto been ignored concerning the composer of *La Wally*, informs me that Catalani was advised to leave Milan due to the unbearable heat of late July 1893. It was recommended he should stay in a sanatorium. The day before he left he wanted to take a bath.

Afterwards, he walked from the baths on Via Annunziata along the long road leading to Via Ippolito Rosellini, located behind Milan's Central Station, where Illica lived.

Red in the face, dripping with perspiration, his brow beaded with cold sweat and shivering from cold, he finally arrived on Illica's doorstep: 'I have come to say my farewells before leaving,' he said. 'You won't forget me, will you? You must carry on working for me! I feel I will only start feeling better once I've written the first notes of *Nella Selva* ... I wanted a bath! It may have been unwise of me ... And it was too hot!' He added, with apparent embarrassment, yet smiling, as though he were trying to dismiss any superstitious fear or foreboding: 'I ended up in Changing Room No. 13!'

He departed – as he said he would – the following morning.[1] He returned quickly, leaving the retreat with its mild climate which was supposed to prolong his life after just a few days. He returned in a seriously ill condition and was tended lovingly by Dr. Ferrario, Arturo Toscanini, who, as we all know, had a deeply fraternal affection for him, and Luigi Illica. He passed away at dawn on 7 August in his home at no. 10, Via Cernaja.

Toscanini and Illica had the sombre honour of dressing the miserable remains and laying Catalani on his deathbed.[2]

---

1 According to Cortopassi this was on 28 July (227), according to Gatti on 1 August (235). Catalani was heading for Faido in Switzerland. See above, p. 75, note 3.

2 The first part of Nappi's article ended here. It was actually Ferrario and Illica who dressed the corpse: see above, p. 77.

The funeral – the grieving, with harsh words from Verdi

EVEN THE holiday season conspired against our poor Catalani. Only a limited number of mourners attended his funeral: Count Ludovico Melzi, the Principal of the Milan Conservatory, Della Porta, the Councillor, Arrigo Boito – whose relationship with Catalani we shall speak of later – Giuseppe Giacosa, Arturo Toscanini, Luigi Illica, Giulio Ricordi, Catalani's students Mario Tarenghi and Carlo Gatti, the Mayor of Lucca, and a handful of others.

Catalani's coffin was adorned with many crowns, including one in bronze from Giulio Ricordi, and those given by his Wally, Ericlea Darclée, his Edmea, Ferni de Gennaro, and Giovannina Lucca. He was buried in the ten-year garden in the Monumentale Cemetery, after the matter had been discussed by the city's Mayor and Giulio Ricordi.[1]

Having been informed of the small number of mourners attending the funeral, and the dearth of orators declaiming the merits of the Maestro, Verdi wrote the following brief and meaningful note:

'*Poor Catalani! He was a good man and excellent musician! How distressing it all is! Do congratulate Giulio [Ricordi] for those few and beautiful words he spoke about that poor man! Shame and guilt upon the others!!*'

The debut – a pianistic disaster

THE FIRST time I met Catalani was at rehearsals for his 'egloga orientale,' *La Falce*, his final exhibition piece performed upon

---

1 Catalani was temporarily buried in the Cimitero Monumentale, Milan; his body was transferred to the Cimitero di Sant'Anna (Cimitero Urbano), Lucca, in March 1894. See above, pp. 77–79.

the completion of his studies at the Milan Conservatory, where he had been awarded his Diploma under Antonio Bazzini. It was a stiflingly hot day in July 1875. The fully-staged performances of the opera were taking place on the suitably adapted small stage of the old hall of the Conservatory.

The delicate demeanour and slender frame of the twenty-one-year-old composer, impeccably depicted in Tranquillo Cremona's masterpiece *L'Edera* ('The Ivy'), made a lasting impression on me.

Catalani himself was on the podium to conduct his work, which he accomplished with lively gestures and energetic baton strokes. I'd heard rumours just moments earlier that 'Catalani has a fever, *he's consumptive.*' Consumption! That wretched word spread from mouth to mouth was to engender preconceived notions in the public's opinion, and ones that, as we shall discover later, were to impinge most deleteriously upon the career of our hapless Maestro.

I saw Catalani once again on the stage of the Conservatory, taking a second bow in front of the enthusiastic audience of the Società del Quartetto Corale, who were enrapt by a performance of the prelude to *La Falce*; and a third time, a year later, in a concert attended by Bazzini. That winter, Catalani conducted rehearsals for some admirable amateur mixed voice choirs, made up in part from Bazzini's composition students and distinguished musicians from our city. They would often cluster around Bazzini and Catalani at the end of the rehearsals, gossiping about the latest important events in the world of music.

Despite being a somewhat mediocre chorus master and choir conductor, Catalani proved to be a man of ample culture. It was at this point in time that we struck up a friendship which was to consolidate over the years. He could not have imagined, and I even less, that I would review his last works.

The following year, 1877, Catalani largely withdrew from social contact, throwing himself wholeheartedly into *Elda*. He would occasionally be seen at the Sunday Recitals given by Carlo Andreoli, his erstwhile piano teacher.[1] Catalani was an excellent pianist, as testified by his few well known and beautiful works for piano, all of which reveal an intimate knowledge of the intrinsic resources of the keyboard. But being of an excessively timid disposition, he was unwilling to play in public, so much so that he only performed once in front of an audience as a favour to Andreoli in the Bach concerto for three pianos with string accompaniment.[2] He performed the third piano part, the second was taken by Giuseppe Frugatta and the first entrusted to the capable hands of Andreoli, who necessarily took the largest part because of the stage fright of the other performers.

It may have been that the work was under-rehearsed, or that the excitement felt by the performers was overwhelming, or possibly that Andreoli had, as was his wont, hurled himself with abandon at the music. Whatever the reason, it so happened that Catalani came in a bar late in the final fugue. Andreoli was hoping that his pupil would skip a bar and catch up with his fellow performers. But poor Catalani completely lost the plot. Andreoli attempted in vain with gestures, eye contact and a gentle word of caution to set him back on track. As he was directing from the keyboard what he should have done was stop the performance and take up the fugue for a second time. But he refused to do so. The audience was obliged to put up with the rather crude result, in which Bach was the innocent party, without protestation; and derived some amusement from the unusual cacophony. They granted plenary indulgence to the guilty party, and Catalani, having engulfed his cohorts

---

1 Carlo Andreoli (1840–1908), a pianist, conductor and minor composer, had been a student at the Milan Conservatory, and was appointed a teacher of piano there in 1875.

2 The Concerto for Three Keyboards and Strings in D Minor, BWV 1063.

in disaster, at the end of all that torture finally scurried off with his tail between his legs to the green room adjacent to the concert hall. He later told me that he had expected to have a thorough dressing down. Yet the admonishment was unforthcoming, possibly because Andreoli felt he could not throw the first stone. All he felt up to saying was: *you weren't destined for a career as a concert pianist.* Catalani took him at his word, not least because he felt he'd been let off lightly. He was never to play in public again.

Elda

MEANWHILE, TO those who asked him how *Elda* was shaping up, Catalani would always respond most evasively. He was extremely capable of steering round a topic of conversation to suit himself, and of diverting his interlocutor's intentions. From the very early stages of the opera's composition no one dared make enquiries because it was blatantly apparent that Catalani did not like to divulge his artistic projects to the world and his wife.

This trait was to stay with him for the rest of his life. He could not bear publicity based on hearsay that was designed for effect. '*A musician shouldn't be an old toothpuller*'[1] I once heard him exclaim when referring to the great hullabaloo, involving the mounting of posters and the publication of numerous newspaper articles, for a new opera written by a well-regarded young composer in the run-up to it being staged in one of our great opera houses.[2]

---

1 I.e. the sort of quack dentist who relies on elaborate advertising.

2 The reference is probably to *Asrael* (1888), the first opera of Baron Alberto Franchetti (1860–1942), which caused a sensation when brought out at the Teatro Municipale, Reggio Emilia. Franchetti came from one of the richest families in Italy, and his opera, industriously promoted, provoked great media interest.

I don't remember Catalani ever inviting critics to his home for a private airing of a new work. Like Verdi, he believed that music written for the opera house should only ever be performed in the theatre. And he was right.

I was, to give you an example, the first to know about his intentions to set *La Wally* to music.[1] He told me about it one winter's evening on Via Manzoni. We were both heading towards the home of his great friend Benedetto Junck to hear a private recital. He told me he was, without exaggeration, completely bowled over by Illica's libretto. Well, I also heard the opera for the first time at its premiere. Catalani did not want anybody at the general rehearsal.

Nor did he deviate from his principles, as some would lead us to believe, when he scheduled the first airing of *Elda* at Turin's Teatro Regio in 1878, the very theatre where later performances were to be held. Giuseppe Depanis attended this first hearing, not in the role of publicist, but as the son and discerning consultant of the Director of the Teatro Regio, who was himself a man of tremendous culture and vision.[2]

Catalani went to Turin at the recommendation of the music publisher Giovannina Lucca to present the work he had just completed to the Director and Maestro Carlo Pedrotti so that it might be christened, as Depanis claims, by a Teatro Regio audience that had not been unsettled by the competitiveness between publishers and conniving fellow composers.

'We were used to receiving proposals, not least because word had it that the Regio was a Mecca for composers eager to have

---

1 It is difficult to take this claim at face value, given Nappi's own account of *La Wally*'s genesis: see below, p. 118 and note. On 20 December 1888 Catalani wrote to Giuseppe Depanis: 'If you want, you can announce in the *Gazzetta Piemontese* (as an exclusive) that Illica and I are working on a splendid subject drawn from a German tale entitled *La Wally*.' Letters 55.

2 Giovanni Depanis (1823–89).

their works performed. We had to listen to all sorts of dross and our woeful experiences had turned us into sceptics expecting the worst,' admits Depanis, who was struck by Catalani's appearance. 'Here was a youngster, who'd only just turned twenty three, and looked it because of his naivety and delicate constitution. *He's catching his soul in his teeth* said the wife of Cichin, the custodian, deeply moved; and the coarse proverbial expressiveness of these words hit the mark.

'The size of the score Catalani placed in front of us on the piano initially destroyed our excellent impression of him: the opera was in four acts and four thick volumes.

'After he'd briefly spoken about D'Ormeville's libretto,' continues Depanis, 'Pedrotti asked him how he'd dared tackle such a difficult libretto. This came as a bolt out of the blue to the young composer, who was totally unaware of the difficulties it presented. He sat down at the piano, and so began the work's first airing. Catalani, a consummate pianist, was afflicted with a crackling, caprine singing voice and he simply found it impossible to play without a vocal accompaniment. Pedrotti, panting with impatience, invited him to stop. But his pleas fell on deaf ears, and minutes later Catalani's crackling voice would once again be heard ruining the performance.

'There followed three hours of mixed punishment and pleasure as we were introduced to the sheer exuberance and beauty of the score. *There's enough music here for two operas!* an enthused but also irritated Pedrotti cried out to a wide-eyed Catalani unsure of whether to take the exclamation as a compliment or not.'

Depanis père took a shine to the youngster, promising to stage the opera as long as Catalani 'lightened certain sections, reworked others, and make no compromises in trimming the work in general.' Yet despite his having taken this advice, cutting and revising the opera quite substantially, Catalani's work was still regarded as too unwieldy when re-submitted to the theatre in 1880.

'Pedrotti, with indomitable courage, made merciless cuts where the maestro had left off. At first Catalani, torn apart in his creative innards, protested; but then he resigned himself to the inevitable. The story behind the rehearsals for *Elda* is legendary in the annals of the Teatro Regio: eighteen cuts were made and a quarter of the score began to disappear bit by bit; and this was after an initial quarter had been cut by the composer himself. It was a salutary lesson for Catalani, and after he'd stopped licking his wounds he felt indebted to Pedrotti for the rest of his life.'

Later works, which are pearls of inspiration, reveal a much more measured approach, such as is found abundantly in the works of Verdi.

Elda was premiered on 31 January 1880 and boasted a sublime cast conducted by Pedrotti, including Nadina Bulicioff, Enrico Barbacini, Edouard de Reszke and Sante Athos.

Depanis writes that this stroke of luck, particularly for a beginner, set jealous tongues wagging, and he adds, for sarcastic effect, that '*music should refine people's behaviour in any situation.*'

Yet as often in Catalani's career, especially in the early years perhaps, he was on this occasion only 'half lucky.' Bulicioff was taken ill the day before the premiere, and Barbacini more seriously as his vocal chords were afflicted. Postponing the opening would have had dire consequences: many of those with tickets for the event had travelled from Milan especially for the premiere; besides, deferrals are always looked upon unfavourably by the public.[1]

Barbacini took the risk and performed under trying circumstances; nevertheless, the trials and tribulations involved in putting on the opera were not to rest there, and the effect was tantamount to the collapsing of a deck of cards. At this juncture I shall hand over to the highly entertaining narrative skills of Depanis:

'The harpist Pinto was about to take his place in the pit when he turned to Pedrotti and informed him that he was feeling

---

1 The second part of Nappi's article ended here.

unwell: he was determined to do his best, but feared he might not make it to the end. Now Catalani, who had always had a special predilection for the harp, an instrument he wrote for with uncommon poetry, had somewhat overindulged himself in writing for the harp in the first version of *Elda*. Given that the orchestra of the Teatro Regio had only one harpist, Pinto was obliged to flit between the pit and stage throughout the entire performance, in order to accompany the singers and choruses.

'A few evenings previously, in a performance of *Poliuto*,[1] Pinto was suddenly taken ill and the angelic harp part was substituted with clarinets at the eleventh hour. This makeshift solution was not suitable for *Elda*, however. What could be done? With a tenor on far from top form, an indisposed leading lady, and a poorly harpist, everyone just went ahead and hoped for the best. *Crazy stuff, this!* grumbled Pedrotti, shrugging his shoulders and saying his beads while making exclamations in a distinctly Veronese dialect. I called for a good, strong bottle of wine to be dispatched forthwith to the rehearsal room, also known as the green room, the one adjacent to the stage, where the performers awaiting their sentence, and in particular where Pinto, in the pauses between his peregrinations, and a pale and worn-out Catalani, could partake of a tot. I spent the entire evening boosting the confidence of the faint-hearted and dealing with the hellish situation, leaving my father to do his utmost with Barbacini.

'We all drew a great sigh of relief as the curtain fell on the closing bars of Act IV: the nightmare was finally over. The first Act and the first half of Act II were enormously successful, the audience cooling off in the second half of Act II and Act III. They warmed up again in the final Act, with Barbacini making heroic efforts to overcome his hoarseness. Catalani and his artists were called three times onto the stage by an enthused audience.'

---

1 Donizetti's opera, written in 1838 and first performed in 1848.

Elda went on to Warsaw and was then laid to rest on the shelves of Catalani's house in Lucca, only to re-emerge ten years later, transformed into *Loreley*.

Dejanice and Edmea

DEJANICE, PREMIERED at La Scala three years later on 17 March 1883, was to suffer a similar, if not worse, fate than *Elda*. Just before the curtain rose the House Manager appeared on stage to inform the packed house that the tenor Edmond Vergnet had lost his voice, yet would endeavour to do his best. Well, he did nothing of the sort. The aphonia was such that he was obliged to perform his role, which was a leading part in the opera, simply by using gestures. The audience, which had not come to the theatre to see a quasi-pantomime, grew more than a little irritated, however much they showed, at the earliest opportunity, their appreciation for Maestro Catalani, and their respect for his music, which unfortunately was turning out to be the seasoning for insipid hokum.

Catalani later confessed that he could easily suffer the torments of purgatory because he'd suffered the torments of hell that evening.

For some time after that it seemed he had retreated from public life. He was known to have entered into a *flirtation* with a young relative of his. Indeed, marriage was hinted at, but it all went up in smoke because of the threat it might pose to his precarious state of health.[1]

Our poor Catalani, so deeply in love, was distraught by the whole affair. His brief prospect of domestic bliss was a dream escaping from his clutches.

Nobody knew the extent of his turmoil. It was probably from this point in time onwards that the full realisation of

---

1 A reference to Catalani's relationship with Luisa Picconi, his cousin. See above, pp. 93–94. Nappi appears to have antedated this by several years.

the potential of his wretched fate dawned upon him. It was as though he were waiting with spasmodic anxiety to be freed from the shackles of torture. Our hapless Catalani was taking each day at a time, waiting for a merciless destiny to say: your day is over!

It begs the question, for whom, and more to the point why did he continue in his work? Was it perhaps for glory? But did he feel that he had enough time to gain her favour?

I turn to Depanis, our ever eloquent and honest narrator.

'Oh, what torment is suffered by one who fleetingly lives through a noble dream and believes himself capable of turning it into reality. His head, spinning with ideas and brimming with optimism, is all of a sudden struck by a flash of lightning: death looms large between his dreams and reality. He is reminded of death by clear and unmistakable signals. He lives one day at a time, fearful that death may strike any day, any hour, any minute!'

My esteemed colleague does well to add: '*The art he worshipped, despite all its disillusions, was his only defence against the pain and cruelty of life.*'

It was art that spurred him on to return to public scrutiny. And with *Edmea* he was once again in the limelight. It was premiered at La Scala on 27 February 1886, at a moment of mad balletic excitement caused by Luigi Manzotti's *Amor*.[1] Possibly it had been chosen because of its brevity, as opposed to the ballet which went on forever. The opera was reasonably well received, but given its melancholic subject matter it never proved a favourite with promoters, despite being a work of considerable

---

1 Luigi Manzotti (1835–1905), the leading Italian choreographer of this period, was famous for his theatrical extravaganzas. *Amor*, on the history of love through the ages, was described by its creator as a 'great choreographic poem': it featured 200 dancers, even more non-dancing extras, and horses and elephants on the stage. It was premiered at La Scala on 17 February 1886, just ten days before the modestly-scaled *Edmea*.

musical worth. When it was performed in the opera houses of Italy it was largely as a result of the efforts of Arturo Toscanini. Will it ever make a comeback?[1]

Loreley

Now we turn our attention to *Loreley*. Catalani had on many occasions expressed his desire for me to attend the premiere of this work, which was to be performed at the Teatro Regio, Turin. He felt, and with good reason, that he had not wasted his time recasting a lot of the material in *Elda* for his latest score. He hoped it would not suffer the same fate as its predecessors, which were languishing on dusty shelves. 'I am convinced,' he would tell me, 'that I have made real progress, and that *Loreley* will be a crowd pleaser, because I have written it with these two fine artists,' touching his forehead and heart.

He insisted on making the point that this new opera was derived from *Elda*. 'I would not like,' he would say to me, 'rumour to charge me with pinching the music from the prelude to Act I of Franchetti's *Asrael*, without his permission, which was, besides, written eight years later. I urge you to consider that the similarities between the two works are entirely fortuitous, because Franchetti, without a shadow of a doubt, had never heard *Elda*.' To me, these words reveal a nobility and refinement of spirit. They demonstrate the respect he had for his colleagues, which was often not reciprocated.

To prove that Catalani was never tormented by jealousy, a weakness that often dims the intellect of musicians when they judge the work of their fellow composers, I reproduce here a very revealing document which honours its author and the artist he was referring to.

---

1 As noted in the introduction, *Edmea* had in fact been revived at Turin in 1910 and Modena in 1914.

For the Colombiane Festival in October 1892 the Carlo Felice theatre in Genoa scheduled *La Wally*, previously only heard at La Scala in the preceding winter season[1] – to follow Alberto Franchetti's *Cristoforo Colombo*. Because of the great success of *Asrael*, Franchetti's opera had generated much expectation and interest in the musical world.[2]

It is easy to imagine Catalani less than pleased about playing second fiddle to a composer who could not boast – despite proving the value of his work – an artistic record comparable to his own. It seems reasonable to suppose that the composer of *La Wally* would instinctively look for even the slightest flaws in the work of this younger colleague, hurriedly attempting the difficult rise to fame.

But this was not the case. As soon as he had heard Franchetti's music, Catalani took up his pen and wrote me this brief and eloquent postcard:

> My dear Nappi,
>   Today I was at the rehearsal for *Colombo*.
> *It's very beautiful music, orchestrated by a great maestro.*
>   Yours affectionately, A. Catalani[3]

Which composer today would do what Catalani did on that occasion?

Let us now return to *Loreley*.

---

1 This is incorrect: as detailed by Pardini, *La Wally* had received 13 performances in Lucca in September.

2 *Cristoforo Colombo* had been commissioned by the City of Genoa to commemorate the 400th anniversary of the discovery of America, and it was always clear that this would be the main attraction of the festival.

3 This note must have been written on 19 September 1892. The following day Catalani wrote to Giuseppe Depanis in identical terms: 'Yesterday I heard the first act of *Cristoforo Colombo* with orchestra. It's very beautiful music, orchestrated by a great maestro.' Letters 117.

Preparations for the staging of the opera were painstakingly slow. Rehearsals came to a temporary standstill because of a seasonal flu that put a large part of the orchestra and staff at the Regio out of action. Moreover, Catalani was not entirely happy with the leading lady chosen by the Directors.

I have in front of me a letter written by Catalani to the Directors at the Regio concerning this very matter. It reveals a tangible respect for his art. He writes, *not in a capricious spirit, but because he is of the firm belief that an honest and sincere artist must be true to himself.* He cannot entrust the role of Loreley to a novice singer *who lacks the maturity to interpret the character and the music fully.*

The maestro does not hesitate in offering an ultimatum to the Directors: *either they find him another artist, or he will have no alternative, painful though it be, but to cancel the performances,* despite his admiration for the conductor Mascheroni and the tenor Eugenio Durot, and knowing that the decision would result in *a moral and material disaster for himself.*

The Directors at the Regio held Catalani in too great esteem not to satisfy his wishes, promptly engaging Virginia Ferni-Germano, who was superb in the leading role.[1]

But there were other complications ahead of the performances. The opera house closed for several days as a sign of respect for Prince Amedeo, who had just died. And, just for a change, Durot was indisposed for the dress rehearsal, so as a consequence the event was held behind closed doors and without the tenor, much to the chagrin of many of the families of the opera house staff, who by rights had always been able to attend.

---

1 On 31 December 1889 Catalani wrote to Virginia Ferni-Germano from Turin: 'Having come here to hear the woman whom they chose for me for *Loreley,* I had to declare that I would withdraw the opera rather than accept her. The administration of the Regio accepted my protest, and while thinking about a remedy, the name of Virginia Ferni came to everyone's lips spontaneously and with enthusiasm.' Letters 72.

Even those who'd taken out a subscription were irked. The opera was being staged towards the end of the season, and there was no alternative other than to schedule the premiere on the evening of 17 February 1890, Dimanche Gras.[1] The public failed to bring with it the cheer of the carnival, opting for the solemnity of early Lent. Here was a stony-faced audience, none too pleased to be attending a serious opera on an evening of festivity. They were tetchy to an extreme and put out by the slightest triviality. The first performance was full of excitement on stage, and produced oscillating reactions from the audience.

The usual malicious crowd was keen to spread the rumour that the opera had been a dismal failure – which could not have been further from the truth – because Catalani, in a demonstration of his unique artistic dignity, both on that occasion and subsequently, refused to take a curtain call. But how can one possibly quantify the success of an opera by taking into account the number of curtain calls?

Catalani was never to enjoy the satisfaction of seeing his *Loreley* performed at La Scala. He was to truly suffer this injustice. He felt he was tolerated, for compassionate reasons only. Wasn't it a known fact that he was suffering from consumption? Isn't that what they said at his debut at the Milan Conservatory?

The public could not bring itself to admit that Catalani had the fibre to produce music with a powerful dramatic quality.[2]

He preferred muted tones; his music had a refinement and delicacy in its contours, and an overriding sense of pathos. He avoided the more vibrant colours of the orchestral palette, sweeping violins and rasping trombones, nor did he make his singers shout. His music could only be perceived as scrupulously sincere and exacting. Many musicians, with greater or lesser sincerity, encouraged this limited view.

---

1 I.e. the last Sunday before Lent.

2 The third part of Nappi's article ended here.

La Wally could not avoid falling victim to these prejudices. I must, for historical accuracy, say that the majority of my fellow critics played an important part in propagating this view by being all too ready in their damning praise. They unwittingly and collectively swayed the public's opinion, much to Catalani's agonising distress.

It was purely by chance that when Catalani, accompanied by Illica, walked into a tobacconist's to buy some stamps, he overheard a heated discussion of *La Wally* in which a two-bit artist claimed in no uncertain terms that as the opera was written by a consumptive, and was indeed consumptive itself, it couldn't be anything other than moribund.

'These wicked words,' Illica rightfully stated, 'were uttered before he passed away; like a merciless sentence, they were engraved on the highly sensitive soul of poor Catalani.'

'We must get on with our new opera, and quickly, quickly!' Catalani exclaimed in the throes of superstitious panic as he left the shop.

The beginning of *La Wally*, and Boito

To QUOTE Illica: 'The person who first glimpsed *Wally*, a Catalani *Wally*, and advised its composer (purely by chance) was Arrigo Boito. It was he who suggested me as a potential librettist for Catalani's new opera. Boito and Catalani enjoyed (and not only because of a deep and reciprocal musical understanding resulting from their work together on *La Falce*) an inevitable and miraculous fusion of soul and mind because of their kindred intellects.'

Reinforcing Boito's suggestion was the advice of friends who also believed that Illica, who'd enjoyed some degree of success in the theatre, and who had a real feeling for all things dramatic, could potentially be a first-rate collaborator for Catalani.

But Illica resisted their advice. He'd already said no to Ponchielli, who had been his piano teacher in Cremona, and who had tried to persuade him to write a libretto, because he found it extremely difficult to find a voice for his characters.

Despite his wariness, a seed of temptation must have planted itself in Illica's soul. But how did it grow?

At this juncture I shall hand over to the librettist himself.

'In those days Arrigo Boito was still living in Via Principe Amedeo No. 1, but not at that time on the ground floor. To get to his apartment you had to climb several flights of stairs, which went on and on and on. *It's not the top floor*, said Boito, *I live in the anteroom of paradise.*

'It was all the way up there, just by chance and through the joy of conversation, that *La Wally* emerged, first from a word to an image, and then from an image to a flash of inspiration.[1]

'Even then the big question for Catalani was the subject matter! His head was awash with so many images and names.'

Illica states that, having reviewed many literary works and authors, Boito exclaimed that there were two writers whose works could not be more musical: Shakespeare and Musset.[2] He justified his claim by saying: *There's already too much music contained in their works, in fact it's all music.*

Illica goes on to say:

'On a typical Milanese summer's day Boito received Catalani and myself into his *anteroom to paradise*, which was in a lamentable state.

---

1 This episode can be fairly precisely dated to August 1888. On 1 September Catalani wrote to Giuseppe Depanis from Montereggio: 'Now a prayer. If you have the *Perseveranza* from last year, I ask you to read a story, translated from the German, entitled *Wally the Vulture*, which appeared in that paper, it seems to me, in the months of July and August. It seems to me that there are strong situations in that story that could lend themselves to an opera libretto. ... I would very much appreciate advice from you, because you intuit some things better than anyone else.' Letters 53.

2 Alfred de Musset (1810–57), French dramatist, poet and novelist whose works inspired around two dozen operas, including Puccini's *Edgar* (1889).

"'You're too high up" quipped Catalani in response to Boito's allusion to the scale – the musical scale. Catalani continued, with a moan, "You're way above the stave!"[1]

'It was then that Boito, with an ascetic gesture, emerged from his room, praising all the top floors in all houses in all climes!

"'When you're this high, my dear Catalani, you belong to the celestial heavens! You're not confined to streets and corridors, houses and prison walls! You won't hear the tramping of feet above your head here, you know! The little angels, the only toddlers who can make a noise up here, have slippers cut from cotton wool clouds; you can't hear them. Here you hear voices shrouded in mystery, not like those down below: *A beautiful new straw hat! ... A scrumptious melon!* Here you get the most amazing firstlings. And the fresh air! You get the tranquillity of dawn, the final russets of the day as it draws to an end, and you've got a swallow for a concierge! Here you get the first lightning, and the earliest heaven-sent teardrops. And the first snow? What it says as it falls – and says with marvellous candour – I hear it clearly, it says ..."

"'The snow!" exclaimed Catalani, interrupting, "The snow is what is so fantastic about life, in its candidness. A woman is like the snow! Full of voluptuousness, yet an ice maiden, too ... yes, this is what women are like!"

'The exchange between Boito and Catalani was tantamount to a love duet; an explosion of adoration for the chaste, pure lady of heaven; a love duet between two poets of love which without question, without us realising it at the time, was prompted by ... the terrible summer heat.

"'Talking of snow," Boito exclaimed suddenly, "*La Perseveranza* has recently published an Italian translation of an intriguing novel by Baroness Wilhelmine von Hillern; a romantic novel. *Wally the vulture*, the central character of the novel, is this wild

---

1 The joke does not work in English. In Italian *le scale* means stairs.

creature, who I see more as raven haired than blonde, because of the nature in which she is immersed. This remarkable heroine lives for art and love. She blossoms and then fades with her art and love, suspended between earth and heaven, wrapped in a white veil of snow. She is surrounded by beauty, and because of her a series of dramatic scenes becomes each more dramatic and vibrant than the last!"'

Both Illica and Catalani wasted no time in seeking out the novel. The clippings of each serialised chapter featured in *La Perseveranza* were read, discussed and moulded for poor Catalani's last opera. Catalani was very happy that von Hillern approved his operatic adaptation, and that she expressed her admiration for his music in an immensely gratifying letter.[1]

Illica tells me nothing about the rehearsals for *La Wally*. Nor does he lay claim to the idea of introducing an interlude at the beginning of Act III, where Catalani's earlier work for strings, the sweet and mournful *A Sera*, is placed.

And what an excellent idea of Mascheroni's and Giulio Ricordi's to perform it with the curtain up.

Catalani himself was keen for the interlude to be performed with the curtain down. He feared that the audience, instead of listening to the softness of the music, might be distracted by the sound of the procession of the village girls returning from the festival at Sölden. He gave in to his advisors' better judgment, and had to convince himself that they were right because the interlude, both then and now, is always rapturously received with the curtain up.

---

1 Catalani subsequently struck up a friendship with Wilhelmine von Hillern, travelling to Germany to see her in 1891, to negotiate the rights for *La Wally*, and again in 1892, to sort out the German translation of the opera. He found her 'really an exceptional and superior sort of woman.' Letters 112. Impressed by *La Wally*, von Hillern even offered to adapt another of her novels as a libretto for Catalani (ibid).

Catalani the teacher

IT WAS a true shirt of Nessus[1] that Catalani had to put on when he was appointed Professor of Composition at the Milan Conservatory.

He found it very difficult, and to make matters worse his financial situation was not very good.

'I don't feel up to teaching,' he would often say to his friends, 'It's all such an effort, teaching is so torturous for me! ... I come home exhausted and can't get back into my own work. But if I can *hit the nail on the head with Wally*' – this was something he said frequently – 'I'll leave the puppet booth and the puppets.'[2] He meant the Conservatory and the students.

Despite this, Catalani was a superb and highly conscientious teacher. His students are unanimous in their praise for him. He never imposed his way of thinking on them.

I quote a letter he wrote to Depanis: 'This year, concerning the Conservatory exams, they've shouted themselves hoarse at me because I let a few of my students indulge a little too much in the so-called areas of the future. I've answered only one thing: if a student of mine feels that way, why should I have to turn him aside? In music, all genres are good, provided that they're *felt and well done*.'[3]

Many of the young composers of today, whom we know all too well, should pay heed to that remark!

When correcting work Catalani would sometimes fall into something like a trance – his students would observe him carefully – and he would maintain silence till the very end. Then,

---

1 A reference to the shirt, poisoned with the blood of the centaur Nessus, that killed Hercules. Figuratively, a shirt of Nessus means a fatal gift.

2 'Lascio baracca e burattini' – a reference to a traditional glove puppet show.

3 Letter of 3 August 1890. Letters 81.

with the utmost sweetness and delicacy, which his students occasionally found excessive – as though he were in fear of offending them – he would make the comments he thought appropriate. He would leaf through, page after page, an orchestral score. Eagle-eyed, he'd immediately spot any flaws or weaknesses and with a few choice words would tackle the crux of the problem. What needed to be changed was a note, a chord, a cadence, an embellishment. After he'd made his observations and suggestions, an intelligent student knew exactly what needed to be done, and acknowledged the fact that their work had turned into something quite different.

Catalani took a personal interest in his students, introducing and recommending them to publishers once they'd completed their course of studies.

* * *

That was the man and the artist. Poor Catalani! Have we given him all the respect he deserves since he passed away? I fear not.

His body, as I said in my account of the funeral, was buried in a ten-year grave. No one sought to arrange a more dignified place of rest. Both Bach and Mozart were to suffer the same fate. Not even a modest stone remains to remind future generations of the composer of *Loreley* and *La Wally*.[1]

It is true a small bronze bust was erected in Catalani's honour in a secluded part of the foyer of the great hall of the Milan Conservatory where concert goers gather before proceeding to their seats. But nobody ever pauses in front of the bust: I can guarantee that very few have cast a lingering gaze upon this monument.

---

1 This is a rather misleading statement – it seems to have been understood that Catalani would be only temporarily buried in Milan, and indeed his remains were transported to Lucca in March 1894, where his grave was marked with a stone. See above, pp. 78–79.

Catalani had a somewhat obscure street in Milan named after him, somewhere in the backwaters of the neighbourhood abutting onto the Buenos Aires district. This is an inadequate homage to the memory of an exceptional artist whose name, I believe, has not yet been admitted to our Temple of Fame.[1]

It was only a few days ago that the idea of erecting a commemorative plaque on the front of the house in which he passed away was considered.

It is most welcome that the monthly publication *Italianissima*, a product of the Association of the *Fratelli d'Italia*, which is currently organising an important concert of Catalani's chamber music to be held in the autumn, has recently mounted an appeal to raise funds to make amends for this deplorable omission. The first list of supporters, published in the 1 August edition, is notably lengthy.

It is hoped that *every single* Italian musician will participate in this fitting tribute to the memory of our illustrious Maestro. I truly wish they will take heed, ensuring that the Italians of tomorrow will never make the mistake of worshipping false idols through blind mass snobbery. May we all aspire to the ideals of beauty, the essence of divine spirit.

---

1 A reference to the *Famedio*, or 'Temple of Fame,' built in 1866 as an entrance to the Cimitero Monumentale, Milan. Many distinguished people connected with the city are celebrated there.

**Bust of Alfredo Catalani
by Achille Alberti (1908)**
(Commissioned by Teresa Garbagnati-Junck, and
formerly in her possession, this is now displayed at the
Palazzo Orsetti, Lucca. Photograph Hans C. Reinders.)

The Sorrowful Star of Alfredo Catalani

Raffaello Barbiera

[Originally published as a chapter in the book
Nella Gloria e Nell'Ombra (1926), pp. 89–96.]

With the demise of Giacomo Puccini a lifeline seemed to have broken. The world needed his songs of love more than ever after so much hatred engendered by the war. I, who had been a longstanding friend, can testify that in that tranquil soul of his were alive the ideals and dreams of love. His young and very unfortunate fellow-townsman, Alfredo Catalani, whose exquisite, noble music was highly appreciated, was another kind soul and genius whose work expressed the essence of what is ideal and divine, sentiments shared by, amongst many others, Massimo d'Azeglio and Heinrich Heine in their memorable writings.

Those who knew Alfredo Catalani intimately, who were familiar with his grace and gentle ways, were accustomed to seeing him pause in mid-conversation as though transfixed by a dream. It was as if his blue-green eyes were staring at something radiant in the distance. There are moments in his ethereal *Loreley*, *Dejanice* and *La Wally* that appear to be created from dream-like reveries.

He once said to me:

'Give me a purely fantastic subject, something that would be poetry in itself.'

'But what about the human aspect?' I replied. 'Human emotions should be depicted on the stage, surely? How can we not portray human beings in opera? Think of Verdi! Where's the fantastic in his work?'

'Well, what about Wagner!' replied Alfredo Catalani.[1] He was smitten with the *Lorelei* legend, versified by Heinrich Heine in a short poem which has been set to music by some forty or so German composers. It is all about the human condition and man's journey towards death! The flaxen-haired temptress sits on a rock bathed in sunset light. There she sings with her celestial voice, combing her golden locks. Her song has a wonderful and bewitching melody, as described in Heine's poem:

> [She] sings a song so free,
> It casts a spell on the gloaming,
> A magical melody.[2]

Her song captivates a helmsman. Heedless of the rocks surrounding him, he gazes up at the source of that enchanting sound. He is absorbed in the music … and the waves engulf him and his boat.

This is the poem. An illusion can make mortals lose themselves?

Two librettists got hold of this obscure subject matter, padding it out with so much fabrication that they changed the original story beyond recognition. I simply do not know how Catalani was able to clothe such an abomination in beautiful

---

1 This conversation, if accurately recalled, is likely to have taken place very early in Catalani's career. By 28 November 1883, in a discussion of librettos with Antonio Ghislanzoni, he was affirming '*Real, human passions*; this is what must be first!' Letters 10.

2 *The Complete Poems of Heinrich Heine*, trans. Hal Draper (Boston, 1982), 76. Barbiera quotes the original German.

melodies worthy of the true legend of the Lorelei of the Rhine; melodies which, unlike the songs of the temptress, save and elevate the opera.[1] They certainly don't let it drown. Puccini was entranced by certain characteristics of the music; and they influenced him.

Apart from *La Falce*, the little one-act opera with libretto by Arrigo Boito that Catalani presented as his end-of-year exhibition piece upon completing his studies at the Milan Conservatory, where he was taught by his beloved and much respected Professor of Composition, Antonio Bazzini, which other libretto of any value was to fall into the hands of this wonderful composer? He was unlucky even in this.

Giacomo Puccini was more a man of the theatre. He chose librettos that worked extremely well on stage. He was more aware of trends, and what the public liked. You only have to think of the subject matter of *Bohème*, typical of its composer, with characters that had never graced the opera stage before, sons and daughters of nature rather than art.[2]

I've already mentioned Antonio Bazzini. He was a spiritual and an artistic father to poor Catalani. He was so proud of his cherished student's lyric gems, of his natural, limpid inspiration, of his pure talent and noble, masterful writing. And he recommended him to the highly intelligent and warm-hearted publisher, Giovannina Lucca.

---

1 The two librettists were Carlo D'Ormeville, who wrote the original *Elda* around 1876, and Angelo Zanardini, who took principal responsibility for adapting *Elda* into *Loreley* a decade later. Barbiera seems to have been confused about their respective roles. Like any number of writers on Catalani, he is also quite wrong to suggest that D'Ormeville somehow developed the libretto from Heine's brief lyric. *Elda* was, without question, adapted from Emanuel Geibel's libretto, *Die Loreley*, originally written for Mendelssohn, published in 1860, and subsequently set by Max Bruch.

2 A short passage is omitted here, entirely concerned with Puccini's *La Bohème*.

It was she who had brought the work of Wagner to Italy, in addition to Gounod's *Faust*, which had failed to please in Paris.[1] It is said that the director of an opera house in Italy once said to an unruly young conductor: 'Look, if you don't calm down I'll make you conduct *Faust!*'

Catalani was from a respectable yet far from wealthy Tuscan family. He eked out a living for himself in Milan by teaching the piano. In order to make things easier for him to compose Signora Lucca paid him a modest monthly stipend, and introduced him to a librettist of hers who had translated some of Wagner's librettos (as had Arrigo Boito).

The librettist was the Venetian and former advisor to the Prefecture, Angelo Zanardini, who simply could not match Giacosa and Boito's beautiful verses.[2] As a man of considerable literary culture and refinement, Catalani was distressed by his colleague's inferior talents, yet he did not know how to go about seeking out a librettist worthy of him. He was, however, to find a peer in the high-spirited Luigi Illica, who introduced him to a novel written by a German writer, turning it into the opera *La Wally*.[3]

It was at this time that the imaginative Alfredo was aspiring to the cloistral peace of a monastic life. He met a distinguished prior who cordially welcomed him with open arms. But the prior was soon to realize that the young man, who vowed to dedicate himself entirely to sacred music, had rather a deep-

---

1 *Faust* had in fact been a considerable success when premiered at the Théâtre Lyrique, Paris, in 1859. Its Italian premiere was at La Scala in November 1862, and it soon became one of the most popular operas in Italy.

2 Zanardini (1820–93), who was from Venice and did translate Wagner, first collaborated with Catalani on *Dejanice* (1883); the context suggests that Barbiera may have confused him with D'Ormeville, Catalani's earlier librettist. Giuseppe Giacosa (1847–1906) was the playwright who co-wrote Puccini's *La Bohème*, *Tosca*, and *Madama Butterfly*.

3 In fact it was Arrigo Boito who first drew the novel to Catalani's attention. See above, pp. 117–20.

seated yearning for artistic and poetic contemplation than the silence of the cloister and the difficult acquisition of true faith and rigorous discipline. It was all to go up in smoke.

Not even that worked out for him! The poet Ghislanzoni, the librettist of *Aida*, lived in the beautiful Barco di Maggianico in a kind of tiny convent.[1] It was there that he received Catalani, asking him to wear a capuchin monk's tunic hanging on a nail in the corridor. It was all a little joke, of course. Catalani felt the need to brighten up his life with a ray or two of sunshine, as despite his youth he was rapidly heading towards an untimely demise.[2]

Moments before a rehearsal was due to start for *La Wally* at La Scala, a pitiful scene took place in the absence of Catalani. The imposing and animated figure of an elderly lady, who was clearly emotional, emerged from the semi-darkness of the stage. It was the publisher Giovannina Lucca.

She made her way to the edge of the stage and amidst the hushed silence of the pit players said in her strong, virile voice: 'Sirs! I appeal to your goodness. This opera, *La Wally*, is original and brimming with fresh inspiration, despite the very serious state of health of our poor maestro. His writing is beautifully descriptive. And you, gentlemen of the orchestra, know it. I beg

---

1 Ghislanzoni was born in Barco di Maggianico, but by the 1880s was living in Caprino Bergamasco, rather complicating Barbiera's story.

2 The relationship between this story and the previous one is baffling. Did Catalani and Ghislanzoni enact a scene in jest that had previously been played out in all seriousness? Pardini seems to have accepted that Catalani did toy with the idea of a monastic life: see above, p. 59. Later, Rinaldo Cortopassi devoted considerable space to the episode, which he dated to 1885, but he seems to have considered the whole business simply a joke of Ghislanzoni's, and in his version there is no suggestion that Catalani had really contemplated a monastic life (140–43). It is unclear whether Cortopassi simply took his information from Barbiera, elaborating and adapting it in his usual fashion, or actually drew on some other source. I suspect the former. For further discussion of the issues between Barbiera and Cortopassi see Michelangelo Zurletti, *Catalani* (Turin, 1982), 67–68.

you: give it all you have got, throw your hearts into it and make sure this opera wins all the success it deserves; may you make an unhappy man happy once again.'

'Yes!' continued the Signora, 'Our poor Catalani may be counting his last days.' She moved away to the accompaniment of mournful mutterings.

The consumption he'd inherited had by this stage ravaged Alfredo's already weak body. His green-blue eyes were shining with the last rays of life.

La Wally was premiered to much positive critical acclaim. Just months later, on 7 August 1893, Catalani died in his apartment in Via Cernaia – an apartment owned by a family that showered him with much affection, treating him like a brother and son.

It was a sad day indeed when, on one of his last visits, he took great delight in an ancient giant beech growing in the gardens under my window, and said: 'I can see everything, but I can hear less and less!' It was the consumption that was sapping away at his hearing, such a precious faculty, and so important to Catalani, a poet of melodies and pursuer of sweet, wandering sounds.

But the heart-sinking sadness I felt at the miserable funeral of our wretched composer was even deeper, nay boundless! There were only a handful of us behind his modest hearse. Not a single representative from the City of Milan turned up, not one. And on the brief journey to the cemetery a renowned poet, who should have felt a kindred spirit, scurried off at the first junction we came to, never to return. Once the coffin had arrived at the colonnade of the cemetery no voice was raised from among the assembled authorities to say something about Catalani.[1] The music publisher Giulio Ricordi made a short, strong speech, and the next day Giuseppe Verdi wrote the following letter to Edoardo Mascheroni:

---

1 This is inaccurate: as Pardini records, Enrico Del Carlo, the Mayor of Lucca, made a speech; there was then a silence, and then Ricordi spoke. See above, p. 77.

'Poor Catalani! He was a good man and excellent musician! How distressing it all is! Do congratulate Giulio for those few and beautiful words he spoke about that poor man. Shame and guilt upon the others!'

The coffin was buried in the cemetery and showered with flowers given by the lady who had a bronze bust cast of her beloved which she donated to the Milan Conservatory. This gentle soul was never to forget her poor Alfredo.[1] Giacomo Puccini subsequently accompanied the coffin to Lucca, where Catalani now lies in eternal peace. The wretched and unspoken enmity that steadily grew between these two rivals was to disappear, I believe and sincerely hope, at the threshold of Catalani's death. And death itself erases and purifies.

Puccini's lucky star shone upon him, and he went from one success to another. Throughout the world his songs of love brought him much glory. Yet a veil of thick darkness was draped over the works of Catalani ... and they lay gathering dust on the shelves of the Ricordi publishing house, which had taken over, upon her demise, Giovannina Lucca's firm.[2] She most certainly would not, with her good heart, have allowed that dust to gather and the veil of darkness to unfurl. But, as is often the case, who takes notice of the dead!

Thirty years after poor Alfredo's miserable fate *La Wally* was finally resurrected thanks to the efforts of Arturo Toscanini, Catalani's former student,[3] who he once introduced to his

---

1 The lady in question was Teresa Garbagnati-Junck. See above, pp. 89–92.

2 In fact Lucca had sold her firm to Ricordi in 1888.

3 A very misleading statement: Toscanini had not been a pupil of Catalani's, and *La Wally* had been revived many times before Toscanini brought it out in his second stint as artistic director of La Scala in 1922. As John Klein has argued, a much more critical moment in the opera's performance history came when Toscanini conducted it to great acclaim in Buenos Aires in 1904: see Introduction, p. 10 and note.

friends with the following fateful words: 'This man will be the world's greatest conductor!' Toscanini was to call his daughter Wally after the heroine of the opera.

Tranquillo Cremona, the pioneering artist, with his wonderfully idyllic compositions which were so in tune with Catalani's genius, almost to a brotherly extent, depicted him in the painting *L'Edera* ('The Ivy'), famous today in many reproductions. The young Catalani is painted by Cremona in the throes of passion. He embraces a beautiful blonde girl who is so sweet, almost heavenly. She is a little fearful, gazing up at the sky, attempting to escape from the fiery clutches of the impassioned suitor who is trying to devote all his love to her with a kiss.

Cremona's painting symbolises the art of the unlucky-in-love Giacomo Puccini. In this canvas the artist is trying to reach for the summit of his ideal, and he can't get there, he never will. It is death that prevents him from doing so.

Carlo Paladini and Catalani's Letters: An Appeal for Information

David Chandler

CARLO PALADINI (1861–1922) was a prominent journalist, music critic, and later political figure from Lucca who, after extensive foreign travels, published the weekly magazine *Il Figurinaio* there between 1889 and 1895. As noted in the introduction, he was a friend of both Catalani and Puccini; he began publishing an unfinished, serialized biography of Puccini in 1903, and in the same year published some of Catalani's letters to Antonio Ghislanzoni and Ferdinando Fontana in an article titled 'A Master of Music and Two Poets of the Theatre: Some Unpublished Letters of Alfredo Catalani' ('Un Maestro di musica e due Poeti da teatro: Alcune lettere inedite di Alfredo Catalani').[1] He felt these letters would be 'of immense importance to the future biographer': 'They are the mirror of his [Catalani's] soul – pure, elevated, and radiant; the soul of an artist and a man; and at the same time a psychological chapter of the utmost interest.'

Paladini's article includes an entertaining account of how he had, by chance, discovered that the letters were in the possession of the celebrated tenor Angelo Masini (1844–1926), who had

---

1 *Musica e Musicisti* 58 (1903), 1041–47.

obtained Ghislanzoni's papers. Paladini persuaded Masini to donate the Catalani letters to the City of Lucca:

> – What would you do if you were in my shoes?
> asked Signor Angelo with a troubled face and the air of a detective.
>
> – Well, I replied very hastily, I'd present the letters of Alfredo Catalani to the City of Lucca ... That way, you can rest assured that nothing will be lost.
>
> Angelo Masini knew how much I loved poor Alfredo, and how much my affections were returned, and ...
>
> My famous friend's face instantly relaxed, in the pleasant, straightforward way typical of people from Romagna; the next day he mailed the precious papers to the Mayor of Lucca.

One must applaud Paladini's desire to see Catalani's letters safely deposited in a public collection. He realized, of course, that there were many other letters in private hands, and included an appeal that those letters, too, or copies, be sent to the State Library, Lucca. This appeal is particularly interesting in that it reveals how seriously Catalani had contemplated basing an opera on the famous novel *Pêcheur d'Islande* (1886) by the French author Pierre Loti (1850–1923):[1]

> At the end of his life, Catalani, with the extreme delight typical of an artist, cherished

---

1 In Catalani's published letters this project is first mentioned to Giuseppe Depanis on 23 October 1892: 'As for *Pêcheur*, I'm studying it with Illica.' Letters 120. A month later, however, he was writing: 'I've set aside *Pêcheur d'Islande*. I need other colours.' Letters 123. The distinguished conductor and composer Leopoldo Mugnone (1858–1941) subsequently composed an opera based on *Pêcheur d'Islande* (*Vita Bretton*, 1905).

the idea of turning Pierre Loti's bejeweled masterpiece, *Pêcheur d'Islande*, into an opera, and for a long time kept up an intense correspondence with the ingenious and original French novelist. They wanted to completely agree on the structure and flow of the libretto. What has happened to the letters of Pierre Loti to Alfredo Catalani? And those of Catalani to Pierre Loti? Has the writer-sailor preserved them?

If this humble article of mine ... happens to fall into the hands of anyone who possesses interesting writings addressed to, or written by, Alfredo Catalani, they would render a great service to the memory of my illustrious fellow-citizen by sending the originals, or at least copies of them, to the State Library of Lucca and its diligent director Eugenio Boselli, to whom scholars and studies of Lucca owe so much.

I humbly make this discreet request above all to Pierre Loti, to whom Giulio Ricordi, with his usual diligent and kindly zeal, will be sure to send this article.

Unfortunately, Paladini's appeal seems to have borne almost no fruit, and even today the whereabouts of most of Catalani's letters is a mystery – a situation which has seriously cramped the study of his life and work. Anyone who looks through Richard M. Berrong's collected edition and translation of Catalani's letters will immediately recognize that the great majority are written to Giuseppe Depanis: and, as Berrong notes, the originals even of those are missing. The letters to Loti, which Paladini was so concerned about, have never been made public; nor have the collections of letters to Alfredo Caselli and Toscanini that

Pardini mentions, and apparently had access to.[1] All the evidence suggests that Catalani was a prolific writer of letters who probably corresponded regularly with at least a dozen people, as well as writing many other letters in connection with specific performances of his operas. Inevitably, some of his letters will have been lost or destroyed; but there must be many still in private hands, waiting to be discovered. Their value to scholars, not just of Catalani, but of late nineteenth-century Italian opera more generally, can hardly be doubted; as John W. Klein noted some years ago, the letters to Depanis alone 'may justifiably be regarded as one of the major and most revealing documents of the two final decades of nineteenth-century Italian music.'[2]

In 2010, then, it seems worth repeating Paladini's appeal from a century ago. If this book comes to the attention of anyone who owns letters written by Catalani, or knows where such letters may be kept, please contact the editor. He will endeavour to ensure that they are published.

---

1 See above, p. 65.

2 Review of Alberto Basso, *Il Conservatorio di Musica 'Giuseppe Verdi' di Torino*, *Music and Letters* 53 (1972), 198.

Catalani on Compact Disc

David Chandler

FOR ANYONE wanting to listen to Catalani's music, the situation is on the whole better than might be expected: most of it has been recorded, mainly thanks to the commendable devotion of the Italian recording company, Bongiovanni.

At least six recordings of *La Wally* have been issued on compact disc, and there has been considerable disagreement over their relative merits. My own favourite is the 1968 studio recording with Renata Tebaldi singing the title role and Fausto Cleva conducting the Orchestre National de l'Opéra de Monte-Carlo. Issued on the Decca and London labels, this has sound that 'is superbly focused and vividly real,' as *The Penguin Guide to Compact Discs* puts it. Criticism has tended to focus on Mario del Monaco's performance as Hagenbach, but the gradual refinement of his singing in the course of the opera, though perhaps not intended, happens to be very appropriate to the role of this rough, tough bear hunter. Tebaldi has also starred in three live recordings, the first and most impressive of which was made at La Scala in 1953 to mark the centenary of the composer's birth (the first recording of the opera), with Carlo Maria Giulini conducting (IDIS 6401/02). Though let down by poor sound, the performance itself is outstanding, and I can do no better than quote David McKee: 'Giulini conducts *La Wally* like the important opera it is. … Giulini's work is marked by masterly interweaving of voices and orchestra, scrupulous observance of dynamics, and extra spring in the rhythms. The result is not a careful performance, however, but a high level of intensity.'[1] Though the recording catalogue is dominated, deservedly, by Tebaldi's interpretations, there is a good alternative in the shape of a German studio recording with Éva Marton in the title role and Pinchas Steinberg conducting the Münchner Rundfunkorchester (Eurodisc RD 69073). The most famous aria from *La Wally*, indeed any of Catalani's operas, 'Ebben? Ne andrò lontana,' has been recorded dozens of times, by all sorts of singers. A DVD recording of the complete opera is expected to be issued soon.

Three recordings of *Loreley* have been commercially issued, though the 1968 La Scala performance with Gianandrea Gavazzeni conducting and Elena Suliotis in the title role has been issued on so many labels that it creates an impression of there being many more. This is a live recording, with bright, somewhat harsh sound, but it conveys great dramatic excitement and conviction. The earlier issues, such as that on the Arkadia label (1992), generally have better sound than the later ones, as well as more generous packaging (including the libretto in Italian); they are worth searching for. There is little to choose between a good version of this 1968 performance and the Bongiovanni recording, a live performance from the Teatro del Giglio, Lucca, of 1982, with thinner, more detailed sound, and more intrusive stage noise (GB 2015/16-2). The Bongiovanni does have the advantage of an English translation of the libretto (albeit a characteristically bad one). The third alternative is a RAI performance from 1953 with Alfredo Simonetto conducting and Anna de Cavalieri as *Loreley* on the Gala label (GL 100.752). A powerful reading of *Loreley*, though let down by poor, muffled sound, it is worth obtaining if only for the bonus tracks of famous singers of the past singing extracts from the opera. A good modern studio recording of *Loreley* is a real desideratum. The ballet from this opera, the Dance of the Ondines, has often been

---

1 'Tebaldi in *La Wally*,' *Opera Quarterly* 13 (1997), 197.

performed separately: the recordings by Toscanini and Richard Bonynge (on his *Homage to Pavlova* collection) are particularly worth seeking out.

In the case of the earlier operas, *La Falce*, *Dejanice*, and *Edmea* just one recording of each has been commercially issued (all by Bongiovanni). Of the three, the *Falce* is the most satisfactory. The performances are a little strained, and the sound a bit harsh, with an echoing, studio quality, but soloists Paola Romanò and Carlo Torriani with the Orchestra dell'Opera Ucraina di Dniepropetrovsk conducted by Silvano Frontalini make a good case for the work that launched Catalani's professional career (GB 2394-2). The recording was made in 2005. The *Edmea*, a live performance recorded in Lucca in 1989 with local chorus and orchestra and Maria Sokolinska Noto, Maurizio Frusoni and Marco Chingari in the principal roles, used a shortened version of the score, and suffers from intrusive stage noise and inconsistencies in the sound. The beauty of the music shines through, especially the absolutely exquisite duet in the third act, which, as Pardini says, 'never failed to bring the house down,' but there is a certain lack of drama, and *Edmea* needs a better case to be made for it. The performance was conducted by Massimo de Bernart (GB 2093/94-2).

The *Dejanice* is the one real disappointment in the series. A live performance from 1985, the soprano who had rehearsed the title role left the production at the eleventh hour, and had to be replaced by Carla Basto, who had insufficient time to learn the part. This led to last minute cuts of important material, and seems to have demoralized everyone concerned, for the performance lacks conviction and hangs together weakly. *Dejanice* is very unforgiving in this respect, for Catalani struggled to surmount the absurdities of the story and the clumsiness of the libretto, by far the worst he set. Though he succeeded, he allowed no room for anything less than a fully committed performance; if one starts to lose faith it is difficult to find it again. Fortunately, a far better version is available to listen to, with Grazia Colli, Gabriella Novielli, Giorgio Gatti, Maurizio Frusoni and Aurio Tomicich as the principals and Arrigo Guarnieri conducting the RAI orchestra. Broadcast in 1975, and privately issued on LP, this is a tremendously powerful performance that brings out the melodic vitality of the opera and allows one to understand why Mahler judged *Dejanice* superior to *La Gioconda*. A number of bootleg copies are in circulation, some of them drastically incomplete and of very low quality. I can supply a properly remastered copy of this recording to anyone interested in obtaining one.

Operas are of course very difficult and expensive to record well, which explains in part why Catalani's non-operatic music has, on the whole, been better served on record. Three recordings can be strongly recommended. Bongiovanni have issued a lovely, warm recording of the early Mass (*Messa per soli, coro e orchestra*), which emerges as a very impressive composition belying its composer's youth and inexperience. It comes complete with the symphonic prologue to *La Falce* and two short choral pieces (GB 2027-2). The ASV label has issued the Quartetto Puccini's lovely, warm-sounding recording of Puccini and Catalani's *Music for String Quartet*, worth getting just for the beautiful adagio movement in Catalani's early and only string quartet (CD DCA 909). The Ducale label issued a delightful recording of Catalani's *Songs* to mark the centenary of his death in 1993. The disc also includes the songs of Giuseppe Martucci, and the performers are Maria Rosa Bersanetti (soprano) and Giancarlo Cocozza (piano). This has become a difficult recording to find, but it is well worth searching for (CDL 017). An attractive alternative recording of six of the songs has been made by Akiko Nakajima (Preiser Records 90647).

Pietro Spada has made a recording of the *Complete Piano Music* for the ASV label (CD DCA 921); though impeccably performed, it is perhaps too understated, and does not compel attention. A rather more powerful and expressive recording of ten of the piano pieces has been made by Simone Soldati (Multipromo MPR022). The orchestral music has fared less well. Most of it has been collected on a Bongiovanni disc with the Warmia National Orchestra conducted by Silvano Frontalini (GB 2097-2). It gives a good impression of the music, but the sound is thin and rather wearying. Far better recordings of the *Scherzo* and beautiful *Contemplazione* are available with Ricardo Muti conducting the Filarmonica della Scala for Sony Classics (the disc also includes orchestral music by Ponchielli and Puccini) (SK 63025). Muti leaves the listener in no doubt about Catalani's consummate skill as a composer for orchestra, and it is much to be hoped that a recording of comparable quality will some day be made of *Ero e Leandro*, Catalani's major symphonic work.

Alfredo Catalani, in his pain, did not rage or cry out
against fate; instead, modestly heroic in his illness,
he was able to reconfirm the ideal superiority of the
human spirit in its work and destiny.
                                        Adelmo Damerini, 1954

Lightning Source UK Ltd.
Milton Keynes UK
04 January 2011
165153UK00003B/9/P